25 Windows into the Soul
Praying with the Psalms

from the writings of

Joan Chittister

Benetvision

25 Windows into the Soul
Praying with the Psalms

Let me tell you about this journal.

It comes out of the prayer life of a living community. It links ancient insight and present circumstance, prayer and personal growth. It will enable you to compare your own reflections to the faith-sharing of others. It will fill your mind and heart with the deepest themes of the Judeo-Christian tradition.

In monastic communities, the Liturgy of the Hours–psalms, canticles and readings from Scripture–are the basic prayer of the day. Every morning and evening, the community gathers to celebrate the presence of God in time, to proclaim their hope in the morning and their faith in the night, to engage in the dialogue of the spiritual life that the meditative listening to the Scripture intends. Monastics are encouraged to memorize the verse of a psalm or of a Scripture reading from the prayer and repeat it throughout the day. These memorized Scripture phrases become the contemplative centering that day as members go from distraction to distraction, from task to task, from meeting to meeting, too pressed to allow themselves long periods of daily private prayer or reading.

This prayer journal invites you to join in this prayer style, a process that monastics call *lectio divina*: sacred reading, reflection, prayer, contemplation and action. You are asked to slowly read and memorize the Scripture, to consider the personal reflections and literary variations that follow each and then to write from your own experience what these words mean to you. You'll see what ideas form the basis of your faith life, what events have brought you to growth, which bother you, which challenge you to think more deeply, which occur again and again, which life insights are just coming to consciousness in you.

This process is divided into seven parts. You can complete them in one reflection period or you can divide each section into seven days.

As the years pass, these psalms and readings from Scripture can shape a contemplative vision that sees the will and face of God in every event, in every human cry from the beginning of time until now. Most of all, this prayer journal is the start of a rich, quiet life of growth in interior prayer that brings peace and faith and reflection and wisdom to the clatter and chaos that is so much a part of modern life. So let's begin. Every one of us can be only as genuinely active as we are contemplative.

Joan Chittister

Window One

Scripture Reading

You will show me the path of life,
the fullness of joy in your presence.

Psalm 16

Read and memorize the psalm verse.
Pray it over and over again throughout the day
until it comes without effort, until it becomes part of you.

Reflection

Pray the psalm verse to yourself thoughtfully several times.
Now read the Reflection and Response suggestion.

The path of life is a sinuous system. We want it to be straight and clear. It very seldom is. It is something that unfolds a little at a time while we're living it. We talk about "planning it" and "finding it" but life is much more often discovered in hindsight than it is in vision. More often than not, we do not find life, it finds us. The only question is whether or not we recognize it and accept it when it comes, whether or not we bring meaning to it and take meaning from it as it is.

Psychologists talk a great deal these days about "alienation," that feeling of being out of touch with the self, of not knowing exactly what we're about in life or how we feel about it or what things mean to us as we race always from one place to the next looking for what we want but cannot identify. Social analysts say that alienation began to mark us as a people when the assembly line began to take the place of craft. People bolted steel frames or sorted peaches or cut pants pockets all their lives but never felt the exhilarating sense of creativity that comes with "building a car," or "growing an orchard," or "designing a suit of clothes."

Clearly, it all comes down to finding "the fullness of joy in God's presence." Maybe alienation is the sign that we are not a secular culture after all. Maybe, in fact, we are a very spiritual one suffering from the fact that we have been cast adrift of all the props and left to find for ourselves the things that really count in life.

Response:
List one or two times when you felt the fullness of joy in God's presence.

Soul Points

Meaning does not come from what we do. It comes from what we are. If we are lovers of beauty, then beauty will fill us all our days. If we are committed to justice, then justice will drive us past all fatigue or failure. If we are devoted to building human community, then we will find meaning in the people whose lives we touch. It's when we are driven by nothing other than our daily schedules that life becomes gray, listless and dour.

Life happens quickly but the meaning of it comes into focus only slowly, slowly, slowly. The challenge is to keep on asking ourselves what it is.

Achievement is what we do for ourselves. Meaning comes out of what we do for others.

Littering is a sign of alienation from the earth. National chauvinism in a global world is a sign of alienation from humankind. Addiction is a sign of alienation from the self. No wonder society is out of kilter.

Beware the day you have no feelings. It is a sign of spiritual sclerosis, of internal death.

Response: Choose one Soul Point and write three questions it raises in you.

Photo Prayer

Pray the scripture verse to yourself several times.
Now pray with the photo.

Response: What does this photo have to do with the scripture verse,

You will show me the path of life,
the fullness of joy in your presence.
Psalm 16

Story
Pray the psalm verse to yourself several times.
Now read the story and respond.

Two disciples, who had become dependent on their teacher, were concerned about what they would do as he grew older and one day died.

The elder, sensing this, drew the disciples near and told them this story:

Once there was a student who was with a teacher for many years. And, when the teacher felt he was going to die, he wanted to make even his death a lesson.

That night, the teacher took a torch called his student, and set off with him through the forest. Soon they reached the middle of the woods where the teacher extinguished the torch without an explanation.

"What is the matter?" asked the student.

"The torch has gone out," the teacher answered and walked on.

"But," shouted the fearful student, "will you leave me here in the dark?"

"No! I will not leave you in the dark," returned his teacher's voice from the surrounding blackness. "I will leave you searching for the light."

Response: What does this story have to do with the psalm,

*You will show me the path of life,
the fullness of joy in your presence.*

Psalm 16

Wisdom Notes

Pray the psalm verse to yourself several times.
Now read the Wisdom Notes and respond.

> The moment of victory is much too short
> to live for that and nothing else.
> Martina Navratilova

> Indifference
> is the invisible giant of the world.
> Quida

> When people are serving,
> life is no longer meaningless.
> John Gardner

> The great business of life is
> to be, to do,
> to do without and to depart.
> John Morley

> What soap is for the body,
> tears are for the soul.
> Jewish Proverb

Response: Copy your favorite Wisdom Note. Why did you choose that one?

Personal Reflection

Write the scripture verse from memory.
Say it aloud.

At this point in my life, this Scripture verse

_____

Action

Do one creative thing this week—bake a cake, paint a picture, cut a bouquet of flowers—that brings you "fullness of joy."

Window Two

Scripture Reading

Happy are those who love God...
they are a light in the darkness
for the upright,
they are generous, merciful and just...
People such as this will be honored.

Psalm 112

Read and memorize the psalm verse.
Pray it over and over again throughout the day
until it comes without effort, until it becomes part of you.

Reflection

Pray the psalm verse to yourself thoughtfully several times.
Now read the Reflection and Response suggestion.

In a century that has spawned Adolph Hitler, Ferdinand Marcos, Nicolae Ceausescu, The Terminator and teenage gangs, on one side, and Martin Luther King, Jr., Dan Berrigan and Mahatma Gandhi on the other, we find ourselves confronted by what seem to be conflicting notions of leadership. Is it force or is it example that defines it? As a result, we have developed some very strange conceptions of what it means to be strong, effective and publicly meaningful. Leadership has become an enigma. Are we to be faithful followers or independent individuals? Are leaders those who are trusted or feared?

The questions are cultural ones. In highly communitarian societies, it is extremely important to foster individualism so that people do not get swallowed up in the name of national development. In these situations leaders become martinets who use people for the sake of personal or social ideals that may or may not benefit the individuals whose lives are ground up in the project. The pharaohs built mighty pyramids but at the price of a million lives. The kings of Spain created a national treasury of American gold but at the price of entire Native American populations.

In highly individualistic societies, like our own, it is just as important to foster a sense of group responsibility so that private interests do not usurp the common good. Corporate executives who take million-dollar salaries for themselves while their laid-off middle-class workers lose their homes to failed mortgages do not benefit society, though they effect it. Street gangs who terrorize neighborhoods to exert a power that is not theirs to use, do not influence a society, they bully it. Family members who manipulate the environment for their own emotional needs, whatever the cost to those around them, control but they do not lead.

Leadership is the ability to pursue the greater good whether anyone else is going in that direction or not. It is, as the psalmist says, the ability to be a light in the darkness for the upright. And it is often a lonely, lonely role.

Response:
List one or two leaders you consider to be a light in the darkness for the upright. Why did you choose these leaders?

Soul Points

Pray the psalm verse to yourself several times.
Now read the Soul Points by Joan Chittister and respond.

Leadership is not an interchangeable part that can be rotated at will. We do not "rotate" organists, computer programmers and accountants. Leadership is a skill, a gift, a charism.

Groups that want to succeed, to survive, need leadership. Groups that kill their leaders, kill themselves.

Real leaders don't set out to organize a crowd. They simply set their faces in the right direction, regardless of how lonely the road, and one day discover that there is a crowd behind them.

It is not necessary to be in an official position in order to be a leader. It is only necessary to be brave, to be honest and to be clear about where you are going and why. Thomas Merton was a spiritual leader who never left the monastery and never gave a retreat. The Beatles led a change in music styles, not by teaching music, but simply by doing something different with it themselves. Rosa Parks had gone to the back of the bus one too many times. The question is a simple one: What is it you believe in that you have failed to do anything about yet? Until you answer that question there is no proof if you are really a leader or not.

"Why is it that wherever Jesus went there was a revolution?" the apocryphal bishop is said to have lamented to his clergy, "but wherever I go, they pour tea." The answer is obvious. Leadership has something do with bringing new

11

light to the dark places in life, not in maintaining old ideas in the name of systemic nicety. As the psalmist says, "people such as this will be honored."

Response: Choose one Soul Point and write three questions it raises in you.

Photo Prayer

Pray the psalm verse to yourself several times.
Now pray with the photo.

Response: What does this photo have to do with the psalm verse,

Happy are those who love God...
they are a light in the darkness for the upright;
they are generous, merciful and just...
People such as this will be honored.

Psalm 112

Pray the psalm verse to yourself several times.
Now read the story and respond.

A young rabbi said to the master, "You know, when I study and when I join others in great feasts, I feel a great sense of light and life. But the minute it's over it's all gone; everything dies in me."

The old rabbi replied: "It is just this feeling that happens when a person walks through the woods at night, when the breeze is cool and the scent in the air is delicious. If another joins the traveler with a lantern, they can walk safely and joyfully together. But if they come to a crossroads and the one with the lantern departs then the first must grope her way alone unless she carries her light within her."

Tales of the Hasidim

Response: What does this story have to do with the psalm,

Happy are those who love God...
they are a light in the darkness for the upright;
they are generous, merciful and just...
People such as this will be honored.

Psalm 112

Wisdom Notes

Pray the psalm verse to yourself several times.
Now read the Wisdom Notes and respond.

A leader is a dealer in hope.
Napoleon

To lead the people, walk behind them.
Lao-Tzu

Where there are no tigers, a wildcat is very self-important.
Korean Proverb

Question authority, but raise your hand first.
Author unknown

Managers are people who do things right,
and leaders are people who do the right things.
Warren Bennis

Response: Copy your favorite Wisdom Note. Why did you choose that one?

Personal Reflection

Write the psalm verse from memory.
Say it aloud.

At this point in my life, this psalm verse

Action

Take one action on behalf of justice, peace or compassion. Become "a light in the darkness for the upright."

Window Three

Scripture Reading

Mercy and faithfulness meet;
justice and peace embrace.
Faithfulness springs from the earth,
and justice looks down from heaven.

Psalm 85

Read and memorize the psalm verse. Pray it over and over again throughout the day until it comes without effort, until it becomes part of you.

Reflection

Pray the psalm verse to yourself thoughtfully several times.
Now read the Reflection and Response suggestion.

This society is locked in mortal combat between mercy and justice. On which side must we err if err we must? Which side do we want for ourselves when we cut corners, bend the rules, break the codes, succumb to needs not being met in other places and ways? Which side is right?

We call the people who argue in behalf of mercy, bleeding-heart liberals. We call the people who cry for more prisons, longer sentences or capital punishment, righteous types. What we never seem to consider, however, is that mercy and justice may be the same thing. What if they can't be separated? Then, what must we do when we judge others? As things stand now, though, we make enemies out of elements that must be inextricably linked if either is to function at all. We make opposites out of elements which, if separated, will each be weakened by the loss of its other dimension. We think that we must be one or the other instead of learning how to be both at the same time.

We forget that it can be merciful to restrain a person from harming either themselves or others. We fail to remember that it can be the highest form of justice to practice mercy. Until, that is, one day we need them both ourselves. Until we examine our own lives and the lives of those we love and find them bathed in mercy where many would have said that justice was required. Then, we understand God a little better. Then we understand both mercy and justice in a different way.

Response: List one or two times in your life when mercy and faithfulness met, justice and peace embraced.

Soul Points

The strangest of all human phenomena, perhaps, is the fact that we all take God's mercy for granted for ourselves but find it so hard to be merciful ourselves. If there were any proof needed that God is completely "Other," this is surely it.

Justice is often confused with righteousness. Justice requires us to take every slightest mitigating factor of an event into account. Justice sees the motive, the might and the need. Righteousness sees only the law.

It is so easy to speak fondly of being merciful to the poor and disenfranchised in the society. What is difficult is to do justice for them because it would require so many changes in our own lives.

To receive mercy from someone else is to learn humility. To extend mercy to others is to learn something about the nature of God. It is very hard to say which learning is more important.

"What are you in prison for?" Mother Jones, the old labor organizer, is said to have asked the poor, young, unemployed man in the cell. "For stealing $50.00," the young man answered. "Too bad you didn't steal a railroad," she replied. "You could be in the Senate by now." It makes you think, doesn't it? How did blue-collar crime get to be the scourge of the nation and white-collar crime just one of the vagaries of business? It is a question worth pursuing, perhaps. The answer could tell us more than we may want to know about our society, about ourselves and about our standards of both justice and mercy.

Response: Choose one Soul Point and write three questions it raises in you.

Photo Prayer

Pray the psalm verse to yourself several times.
Now pray with the photo.

Response: What does this photo have to do with the psalm verse,

Mercy and faithfulness meet;
justice and peace embrace.
Faithfulness springs from the earth,
and justice looks down from heaven.

Psalm 85

Story

Pray the psalm verse to yourself several times.
Now read the story and respond.

"Who is closer to God," the seeker asked, "the saint or the sinner?"

"Why, the sinner, of course," the elder said.

"But how can that be?" the seeker asked.

"Because," the elder said, "everytime a person sins they break the cord that binds them to God. But every time God forgives them, the cord is knotted again.

And so, thanks to the mercy of God, the cord gets shorter and the sinner closer to God."

Response: What does this story have to do with the psalm,

Mercy and faithfulness meet;
justice and peace embrace.
Faithfulness springs from the earth,
and justice looks down from heaven.

Psalm 85

Wisdom Notes

Pray the psalm verse to yourself several times.
Now read the Wisdom Notes and respond.

Children are innocent and love justice,
while most adults are wicked and prefer mercy.
G.K. Chesterton

When others are weeping blood, what right have I to weep tears?
José Marti

Injustice never rules forever.
Seneca

Justice...limps along, but it gets there all the same.
Gabriel Garcia Marquez

Humankind's true moral test, its fundamental test
(which lies deeply buried from view),
consists of its attitude towards those who are at its mercy: animals.
And in this respect humankind has suffered a fundamental debacle,
a debacle so fundamental that all others stem from it.
Milan Kundera

Response: Copy your favorite Wisdom Note. Why did you choose that one?

Personal Reflection

Write the psalm verse from memory.
Say it aloud.

At this point in my life, this psalm verse

_____

Action

Volunteer at a service or donate to a group "where mercy and faithfulness meet." For example, a soup kitchen that feeds the hungry and speaks out against poverty, or a community-supported agriculture system that uses renewable energy.

Window Four

Scripture Reading

Send your light and your truth;
let these be my guide.
Lead me to your holy mountain,
to the place where you dwell.

Psalm 43

Read and memorize the psalm verse.
Pray it over and over again throughout the day
until it comes without effort, until it becomes part of you.

Reflection

Pray the psalm verse to yourself thoughtfully several times.
Now read the Reflection and Response suggestion.

The dark spots in life–those times when the present seems unbearable and the future seems impossible–seem often to be empty, useless moments. It's only later, when we look back, that we can see how really rich those periods were for us. Darkness, in fact, is the beginning of light. It is the one place where we are obliged to see what we have never been willing or able to understand before. Darkness is spiritual ambiguity, holy contradiction, disarming mystery. The one major function of darkness in this world, whatever kind of darkness it may be, is always, in the final analysis, enlightenment. What we learn when we cannot see our way through a hard place in life are insights that we have failed to discern in better situations. When life is good we don't look as closely, perhaps. When life is easy, we don't listen at all. When life is difficult, we have the sense to wonder why. We hear a great deal about loss in life, for instance, but we never really come to know intangible presence until someone we really love dies. We read one article after another on simplicity of life but we never really come to realize how little it takes to be happy until we lose something of great significance. Enlightenment is the moment in life when we have little left outside ourselves and suddenly discover something inside ourselves that compensates for all of it.

Philosophers and theologians debate eternally what every human being, one way or another, comes to know without doubt: Life is a process of watching the material dimensions of the human condition slip away while the spirit grows stronger, greater, richer all the way to eternity. All the while our bodies wane, the spirit is waxing. It is the paradox of life. That's why no one is ever ready to die. The older we get the more we are just beginning to understand life and to really live it well. That process is called enlightenment.

Response: List one or two times in the past month when you have felt at home, in the place where God dwells.

Soul Points

Pray the psalm verse to yourself several times.
Now read the Soul Points by Joan Chittister and respond.

There are moments in life when everything we've ever worked for, waited for, planned for, saved for, crumbles and dies and fails. The job goes, the money runs out, a child dies, the family breaks down, the business collapses, the dreams of a lifetime break into pieces. Darkness is the feeling. Despair is the temptation. Freedom is the hope. If I can just cling to life trustingly, that is enlightenment. After that, there is nothing whatsoever I can ever lose again that can destroy me.

Jonathan Swift wrote, "May you live all the days of your life." How rare that is. Most of us live half of today waiting for some nebulous tomorrow instead of enjoying what is in front of us right now.

The mystic Mechtild of Magdeburg defines enlightenment best, I think. She says that the purpose of life is to see God in all things and all things in God. When that happens there is no darkness left.

The psychologist Carl Jung tried to teach the world that there was a light side and a dark side, a dark side and a light side to everything. No matter where you are in life now, in darkness or in light, enlightenment involves considering what its opposite would demand of us. Then, we'll know what life will require of us to complete the present process.

How shall we recognize enlightenment? Enlightenment is the moment at which the need for things falls away. Enlightenment is the moment at which we put the great hurts of life behind us and embrace the new with all our energy, with all our heart. Enlightenment is the moment at which we discover that the fullness of life is in the first great music we are able to hum, the first flower bud we look for and find, the first friend we love without expecting to be loved in return.

Response: Choose one Soul Point and write three questions it raises in you.

Photo Prayer

Pray the psalm verse to yourself several times.
Now pray with the photo.

Send your light and your truth;
let these be my guide.
Lead me to your holy mountain,
to the place where you dwell.

Psalm 43

Response: What does this photo have to do with the psalm verse?

Pray the psalm verse to yourself several times.
Now read the story and respond.

"Master, I come to you seeking enlightenment," the priest said to the Holy One.

"Well, then," the master said, "for the first exercise of your retreat, go into the courtyard, tilt back your head, stretch out your arms and wait until I come for you."

Just as the priest arranged himself in the garden the rain came. And it rained. And it rained. And it rained.

Finally, the old master came back. "Well, priest," he said. "Have you been enlightened today?"

"Are you serious?" the priest said in disgust. "I've been standing here with my head up in the rain for an hour. I'm soaking wet and I feel like a fool!"

And the master said, "Well, priest, for the first day of a retreat that sounds like great enlightenment to me."

Response: What does this story have to do with the psalm,

Send your light and your truth;
let these be my guide.
Lead me to your holy mountain,
to the place where you dwell."

Psalm 43

Wisdom Notes

Pray the psalm verse to yourself several times.
Now read the Wisdom Notes and respond.

Do not think you will necessarily be aware of your own enlightenment.
Dogen

To live fully, outwardly and inwardly,
not to ignore external reality for the sake of the inner life,
or the reverse–that's quite a task.
Etty Hillesum

Do not seek illumination unless you seek it as a man whose hair is on fire.
Sri Ramakrishna

For everything that lives is holy, life delights in life.
William Blake

Discovery consists of seeing what everybody has seen
and thinking what nobody has thought.
Albert Szent-Gyorg

Response: Copy your favorite Wisdom Note. Why did you choose that one?

Personal Reflection

Write the psalm verse from memory.
Say it aloud.

At this point in my life, this psalm verse

Action

Do at least one thing today that nourishes your soul, that "leads you to God's holy mountain, to the place where God dwells."

Window Five

Scripture Reading

Caught up in your beauty,
I speak of my heart's desire;
to find the fullness of life,
dwelling in your presence forever.

Psalm 27

Read and memorize the psalm verse.
Pray it over and over again throughout the day
until it comes without effort, until it becomes part of you.

Reflection

Pray the psalm verse to yourself thoughtfully several times.
Now read the Reflection and Response suggestion.

A sixth century document, *The Rule of Benedict*, designed to point the way to fullness of life, is quite clear: Everybody must be known by somebody wise enough, caring enough, balanced enough to help them know themselves. Benedict calls it the Fourth Degree of Humility. The implication is that if we fail to work through the thoughts, the ideas, the pains that consume us we can't grow beyond them. We need to learn to trust, to share, to admit our weaknesses, to take off our masks, to be in the world with honesty and authenticity.

That doesn't mean that we tell everyone everything. It means that we must tell someone everything. That's why choosing friends is so important. That's why allowing someone into our lives is key to our own development. Intimacy is not a condition, it is a necessity of human growth.

"I felt it shelter to speak to you," Emily Dickinson wrote. Perhaps there is no better way to describe the real effects of intimacy. Those who are our intimates are those with whom we are safe and respected, regardless how small we may seem to ourselves at the time. The question is whether or not any of us have ever fully lived until we have known such comfort.

We are not, the psalmist is clear, a world unto ourselves. To find the fullness of life, we must go out of ourselves to find the Divine Presence in the other. The awareness of beauty beyond ourselves calls us to become more than we can possibly be alone.

Response: Name one or two people whom you would describe as intimate friends. Thank God for them.

Soul Points

We can only be intimate with those whom we allow to be themselves. Intimacy is not the right to control another; it is simply the expectation that we can trust the other in our behalf. The person with whom we can be intimate, we may tell the other half of our soul knowing that it will never under any circumstances be used against us and that they can do the same with us.

If there is no one in life with whom you are completely honest–completely– then there is no one in life you really love.

Beware people who won't give you space for more friends, other activities, new ideas and unrelated experiences. They are a lot more interested in themselves than they are in you.

The painter Claude Monet wrote: "I perhaps owe having become a painter to flowers." There's a lesson in that statement, I think. Do you love anything else enough to say that it has truly changed, shaped, formed your own life?

Intimacy is that point in a relationship when another person knows me at least as well as I know myself and accepts what they see without judgment. It does not imply that they accept in me less than everything of which I'm capable.

Response: Choose one Soul Point and write three questions it raises in you.

Photo Prayer

Pray the psalm verse to yourself several times.
Now pray with the photo.

Response: What does this photo have to do with the psalm verse,

Caught up in your beauty,
I speak of my heart's desire;
to find the fullness of life,
dwelling in your presence forever.

Psalm 27

Pray the psalm verse to yourself several times.
Now read the story and respond.

There lived a person renowned for his wisdom and holiness. Whenever he was asked how he had become so enlightened, he said, "I know what is in the Bible."

One day he had just given this answer to an inquirer when an exasperated voice shouted, "Well, what is in the Bible?"

"In the Bible," said the Enlightened One, "there are two pressed flowers and a letter from my friend, Jonathan."

Response: What does this story have to do with the psalm,

Caught up in your beauty,
I speak of my heart's desire;
to find the fullness of life,
dwelling in your presence forever.

Psalm 27

Wisdom Notes

Pray the psalm verse to yourself several times.
Now read the Wisdom Notes and respond.

Let there be space in your togetherness.
Kahlil Gibran

Love from one being to another can only be that two solitudes come nearer,
recognize and protect and comfort each other.
Han Suyin

Am I united with my friend in heart/
What matters if our place be wide apart?
Persian poet Anwar-I-Suheili

Sometimes our light goes out, but it is blown again into flame
by an encounter with another human being.
Each of us owes the deepest thanks to those who have rekindled this light.
Albert Schweitzer

If you press me to say why I loved him,
I can say no more than it was because he was he, and I was I.
Montaigne

Response: Copy your favorite Wisdom Note. Why did you choose that one?

Personal Reflection

Write the psalm verse from memory.
Say it aloud.

At this point in my life, this psalm verse

Action

Take a chance today, risk who you are by having a meaningful conversation
with another person. Truly "speak of your heart's desire."

Window Six

Scripture Reading

As parents are tender with their children,
so God is gentle with those who believe.

Psalm 103

Read and memorize the psalm verse.
Pray it over and over again throughout the day
until it comes without effort, until it becomes part of you.

Reflection

Pray the psalm verse to yourself thoughtfully several times.
Now read the Reflection and Response suggestion.

"Family" is a very different, a very difficult, concept for us in this culture today. We have been raised, many of us, in a society of uniracial, one-denominational families where fathers were the "breadwinners" and mothers were "housewives," where colors did not mix and women as a class were economically dependent. Divorce was socially unacceptable. Women were legal minors. Childbearing was a basically uncontrollable process. It was our ideal of the perfect home. But, as a result, many children lived in loveless, violent homes from which there was no escape.

We mourn the loss of those ideal structures and, for many reasons, rightly so. The number of single-parent homes is on the increase. The number of merged families leaves children with two part-time families rather than one full-time family. Childhood poverty is multiplying at an alarming rate in the richest country in the world. Marriage, in too many cases, has become a very tentative venture. We are inclined, as a result, to see earlier forms of family life as perfect, despite the fact that those periods, too, produced great suffering, even great sin. People lived in loveless marriages all their lives. Children were unwanted, ignored, abused and deprived. Women and children were abandoned with impunity, made poor or forced to cope with countless infidelities. Whether the ideal was ever truly real becomes a question of great social import.

At the same time, we have been so concerned about the emergence of various forms of modern families–biracial, single parent, merged, mixed, blended and single sex that we have too often lost sight of the underlying essence of human relationships. When we pray, "God of Love," we forget that God's love takes no form, has no boundaries, knows no barriers, requires no systemic litmus test of propriety. We forget that God's love is unconditional and so requires the same of us. We have forgotten that only love can make a family.

But the psalmist knows better. The psalmist talks only and always of the God who is tender, the God who brooks no obstacles to covenant, the God who bars no color, no status, no social caste, no sex from the fullness of life because this God puts love above law. The psalmist makes us examine every relationship for the quality that maintains it, not the legalities that define it or the structures that shape it.

If we are to become God's family, the human family, we must surely do the same, praying only that every family, whatever its form, will have the resources it needs to live in dignity and in love and the spirituality it needs to live with integrity, tenderness and laughter always.

Response: Make a list of five family members (immediate or other) who are lonely, estranged, hurt, ashamed, angry, etc. Now reach out in some way.

Soul Points

Pray the psalm verse to yourself several times.
Now read the Soul Points by Joan Chittister and respond.

"Making the decision to have a child," Elizabeth Stone wrote, "is momentous. It is to decide forever to have your heart go walking around outside your body." And she was correct but incomplete in the concept. All children, whether ours or not, are the carriers of the life we leave behind for them. In every living child there resides the consequences of the policies, the consciences of us all.

☞

There is a child in all of us who needs to be protected, cared for, nurtured, valued. Who takes care of the child in you–and whose soul child are you loving to life? Whoever it is, the soul child is really your family–regardless to whom you are legally related.

☞

There are families everywhere struggling with their family's secret poverty, division, alcoholism, abuse and smiling, smiling, smiling on the outside. Open your arms today. Take everyone in. Half the people you see are bearing a secret too big for them to bear alone.

☞

Don't ever be afraid to be tender. Tenderness is a bond thicker than blood, surer than eternity, more promising than power. Tenderness says that we are looking for another and have ourselves been found.

☞

It's amazing the things that we allow to wrench families apart: religion, marriage, homophobia, jealousy, money. That's like fighting over crumbs at a banquet table.

Response: Choose one Soul Point and write three questions it raises in you.

Photo Prayer

Pray the psalm verse to yourself several times.
Now pray with the photo.

Response: What does this photo have to do with the psalm verse,

As parents are tender with their children,
so God is gentle with those who believe.

Psalm 103

Story

**Pray the psalm verse to yourself several times.
Now read the story and respond.**

The great Japanese poet, Ryokan, was asked by his brother to come to his house and speak to his delinquent son.

Ryokan came and did not say a word of admonition to the boy. He stayed overnight and prepared to leave the next morning.

As the wayward nephew was lacing up Ryokan's sandals, he felt a drop of warm water. Glancing up, he saw Ryokan looking down at him, his eyes full of tears. Ryokan then returned home, and the nephew changed for the better.

Response: What does this story have to do with the psalm,

*As parents are tender with their children,
so God is gentle with those who believe.*

Psalm 103

Wisdom Notes

Pray the psalm verse to yourself several times.
Now read the Wisdom Notes and respond.

Home is the place where, when you go there,
they have to take you in.
Robert Frost

Teach your children what we have taught our children,
that the earth is our mother.
Whatever befalls the earth befalls the sons and daughters of the earth.
This we know.
All things are connected like the blood which unites one family.
Chief Seattle

Children are our most endangered species.
Daniel Berrigan

Nothing you do for a child is ever wasted.
Garrison Keillor

I am part and parcel of the whole
and cannot find God apart from the rest of humanity.
Gandhi

Response: Copy your favorite Wisdom Note. Why did you choose that one?

Personal Reflection

Write the psalm verse from memory.
Say it aloud.

At this point in my life, this psalm verse

Action

Do something special for a child today, your own child, a nephew or niece, a grandchild, a child caught in poverty, a child of a single parent. Do something tender with a child, be as gentle as God.

Window Seven

Scripture Reading

*God is the Creator of all the earth,
caring for all nations.*

Psalm 47

Read and memorize the psalm verse.
Pray it over and over again throughout the day
until it comes without effort, until it becomes

Reflection

Pray the psalm verse to yourself thoughtfully several times.
Now read the Reflection and Response suggestion.

There are two concepts in US history that deserve to be revisited in these times. The first is "patriotism." The second is "jingoism." They are not synonyms, much as we are sometimes inclined to make them. Patriotism is love of country, literally the "father"land. Jingoism is chauvinism, a love of country that lacks a critical eye. Or better yet, perhaps, a love of country that lacks a loving eye. When we love something to such a degree that we lose the capacity to compare it to its own best potential, we don't really "love" it at all. We idolize it.

Jingoism is destructive idolatry, the kind of national fetish which can, if taken to its limit, end in the holocaust of Jews, the genocide of Bosnians, the decimation of Palestinians and the massacre of Native Americans. But the psalmist is clear. God "cares for all nations." What we do in the name of "Americanism" to people will be weighed in the light of what is good for all creation, our own and those whose lives as a nation we touch.

Patriotism, on the other hand, is a commitment to the ideals for which, as a people, we say we strive. Real patriotism welcomes, encourages, commits itself to the great national debates that question war, resist taxes, and determine penal systems.

Patriotism asks hard questions: Are we really putting enough money into education in this country? Is eight weeks of training enough to provide people on welfare with the skills they need to find and maintain employment after we have cut off food stamps to their children? What exactly does an ethic of life require at all levels, at all times? Should we still be putting over half the national budget into the military establishment? Those questions engage the patriot with honesty and courage. Those questions and others just as difficult, just as scalding, will determine the real direction of this country.

Response: List five ways that you care for all the nations.

Soul Points

Real patriotism will not be reached on this planet until, for each of us, our country is the world. Until then, we are all merely tribes fighting for territory that doesn't belong to us in the first place.

⤿

It is only when we travel outside our country that we can really come to know what it means to be from the US. It is an exhilarating and humiliating thing. Real love of country demands that we find the beauty in other cultures and strive to grow from what we learn from others. As Albert Camus says, "I love my country too much to be a nationalist."

⤿

Cory Aquino, liberating president of the Philippines, said something to me in her presidential office that seared my soul: "You Americans have two civil rights policies," she said. "One you apply inside your country; the other you apply to everyone else." I've never been able to forget it. What do you think that's saying? What does it have to do with patriotism?

⤿

The philosopher José Ortega y Gasset wrote: "What makes a nation great is not primarily its great men and women, but the stature of its innumerable mediocre ones." That's us. We're the ones who are responsible for the character of this country. Every time I hear someone say, "Well, you have to assume that the politicians know best what to do," I realize that one more person has surrendered citizenship for childish obedience.

⤿

The spirituality of patriotism demands that we "render unto Caesar the things that are Caesar's" and not one thing more.

Response: Choose one Soul Point and write three questions it raises in you.

Photo Prayer

Pray the psalm verse to yourself several times.
Now pray with the photo.

Eleanor Roosevelt

Response: What does this photo have to do with the psalm verse,

God is the Creator of all the earth,
caring for all nations.

Psalm 47

**Pray the psalm verse to yourself several times.
Now read the story and respond.**

During World War II a German widow hid Jewish refugees in her home. As her friends discovered the situation, they became extremely alarmed.

"You are risking your own well-being," they told her.

"I know that," she said.

"Then why," they demanded, "do you persist in this foolishness?"

Her answer was stark and to the point. "I am doing it," she said, "because the time is now and I am here."

Response: What does this story have to do with the psalm,

*God is the Creator of all the earth,
caring for all nations.*

Psalm 47

Wisdom Notes

Pray the psalm verse to yourself several times.
Now read the Wisdom Notes and respond.

I don't measure America by its achievement,
but by its potential.
Shirley Chisholm

I'm a universal patriot, if you could understand me rightly:
my country is the world.
Charlotte Brontë

I tremble for my country when I reflect that God is just.
Thomas Jefferson

True patriotism hates injustice in its own land more than anywhere else.
Clarence Darrow

You're not supposed to be so blind with patriotism
that you can't face reality.
Wrong is wrong, no matter who does it or who says it.
Malcolm X

Response: Copy your favorite Wisdom Note. Why did you choose that one?

Personal Reflection

Write the psalm verse from memory.
Say it aloud.

At this point in my life, this psalm verse

Action

Spend thirty minutes today learning about a culture or religion you fear or don't understand. Begin and end your study time with the psalm verse "God is the Creator of all the earth, caring for all nations."

Window Eight

Scripture Reading

Guardian of the orphan,
defender of the widowed,
such is God, who gives
the lonely a home.

Psalm 68

Read and memorize the psalm verse.
Pray it over and over again throughout the day
until it comes without effort, until it becomes part of you.

Reflection

Pray the psalm verse to yourself thoughtfully several times.
Now read the Reflection and Response suggestion.

I was a very small child, about four years old, when it happened. Rain had beat against our house for the entire day. Sitting at our living room window, lost in the kind of rainy-day reveries common to an only child, and counting raindrops for hours, I saw him come out of the woods on the other side of the road. The boy was thin, bedraggled, dirty and soaking wet. He was also miles away from anywhere. I watched him crouch under our porch steps while the day got darker and darker. He never moved. I shuddered at the sight of him and went for my mother. I don't remember the rest of the details. I only remember him sitting at our kitchen table in my father's clothes, head down, his hands strung limp in his lap as my mother ladled more soup into his bowl and spread more jam on his bread. Then they came in uniforms and took him slowly away as I watched from the safety of distance. When he left, he hugged my mother. She put her arms around him and kissed him on the head. Who was this stranger who had usurped my mother's love? And why? I have never forgotten the scene.

It doesn't take a lot of thinking to understand why qualities like honesty, self-control, devotion and love are components of the spiritual life. But hospitality–the fine art of being nice to people? Why–of all things–hospitality? The question captures the imagination of the soul. It gives us something worth thinking about, perhaps. Why is it that one of the oldest spiritual documents in Western civilization, *The Rule of Benedict*, says hardly a word about asceticism but speaks over and over again about hospitality and the reception of guests? It's a conundrum that teases us with an insight worth having.

The answer, I think, is that hospitality is basic. It's what teaches us about all the other things in life. It's what prepares us to deal with all the other things. It's hospitality that teaches us honesty and self-control, devotion and love, openness and trust. The way of hospitality is more difficult and more meaningful than any asceticism we could devise for ourselves.

Desert monastics, spiritual seekers who went into the backwaters of Egypt and the Middle East to live a life of solitude and prayer, broke every rule they lived by on behalf of hospitality because to allow a person to wander through a desert without water and without help is, in the final analysis, to condemn them to death. Hospitality is the fine art of having an open soul and a listening mind in a world where, alone, we would all die from starvation of the soul.

Response: Think of the person you trust least, care for least, in life. Now, in your mind's eye, bring them into your space, offer them your food, sit in perfect silence and let them talk. How do you feel about them now? Funny how talk changes things, isn't it?

Soul Points

Pray the psalm verse to yourself several times.
Now read the Soul Points by Joan Chittister and respond.

It's so easy to be nice to neighbors. It's when people come into the neighborhood that we've never seen before–the Afro-American who's taking a walk; the Muslim who's looking at the houses; the bag lady wandering through town that the human heart is taxed to the ultimate. "If we are gracious and courteous to strangers," Francis Bacon wrote, "it shows that we are citizens of the world."

Scripture is a catalog of messages from God that come through strangers. One Scripture story after another details the blessings that come in the unexpected. The thought gives a person pause. Could it be that every stranger turned away is a divine message missed?

Hospitality is not simply a matter of opening the door; it is a matter of opening the heart.

"If you stop to be kind," Mary Webb wrote, "you must swerve often from your path." Yes, but imagine all the scenery you'll see on the way that you never would have otherwise, all the roads you'll take that you never knew existed, all the places you'll come to in life that you could otherwise have missed, all the people you'll meet whom you would never have seen had you hurried through life. Hospitality may take us where we would not go, perhaps, but always to our own great good.

Hospitality is the way we turn a prejudiced world around, one heart at a time.

When I let strange people and strange ideas into my heart, I am beginning to shape a new world. Hospitality of the heart could change US domestic policies. Hospitality of the heart could make my world a world of potential friends rather than a world of probable enemies.

Response: Choose one Soul Point and write three questions it raises in you.

Photo Prayer

Pray the psalm verse to yourself several times.
Now pray with the photo.

Response: What does this photo have to do with the psalm verse,

Guardian of the orphan, defender of the widowed,
such is God, who gives the lonely a home.

Psalm 68

Story
**Pray the psalm verse to yourself several times.
Now read the story and respond.**

An old rabbi once asked his pupils how they could tell when the night had ended and the day had begun.

"Could it be," asked one of his student, "when you can see an animal in the distance and tell whether it's a sheep or a dog?"

"No," answered the rabbi.

Another asked, "Is it when you can look at a tree in the distance and tell whether it's a fig tree or a peach tree?"

"No," answered the rabbi.

"Then when is it," the pupils demanded.

"It's when you can look on the face of any man or woman and see that it is your sister or brother. Because if you cannot see this, it is still night."

Response: What does this story have to do with the psalm,

Guardian of the orphan,
defender of the widowed,
such is God,
who gives the lonely a home.

Psalm 68

Wisdom Notes

Pray the psalm verse to yourself several times.
Now read the Wisdom Notes and respond.

Receive the guest as Christ.
the sixth century *Rule of Benedict*

In Vietnam there is a traditional folk image
of the difference between heaven and hell.
In hell people have chopsticks a yard long
so that they cannot reach their mouths.
In heaven, the chopsticks are the same length
but the people feed one another.

Grant me to recognize in other men and women, my God,
the radiance of your own face.
Teilhard de Chardin

Give me your tired, your poor,
your huddled masses yearning to breathe free,
the wretched refuse of your teeming shore.
Send these, the homeless, the tempest-tossed to me,
I lift my lamp beside your golden door.
Emma Lazarus (on the Statue of Liberty)

My candle burns at both ends/ it will not last the night./
But ah, my foes, and oh, my friends–/ it gives a lovely light!
Edna St. Vincent Millay

Response: Copy your favorite Wisdom Note. Why did you choose that one?

Personal Reflection

Write the psalm verse from memory.
Say it aloud.

At this point in my life, this psalm verse

Action

Do an act of hospitality today for a neighbor: rake their leaves, shovel the
sidewalk, take them a dessert, offer to babysit....

Window Nine

Scripture Reading

Though I walk in the valley of darkness,
no evil do I fear.
Your rod and staff comfort me.

Psalm 23

Read and memorize the psalm verse.
Pray it over and over again throughout the day
until it comes without effort, until it becomes part of you.

Reflection

Pray the psalm verse to yourself thoughtfully several times.
Now read the Reflection and Response suggestion.

Once upon a time, an old Hasidic tale teaches us, the local Jewish congregation was very concerned about the fact that their rabbi disappeared into the forest every single Sabbath night. Was he chanting with angels? Was he praying with Elijah? Was he communing directly with God? So, after months of this, they finally sent someone to follow him who would report back to them on where he was going. Sure enough, the next Sabbath eve, the rabbi went through the woods, up a mountain path, over the crest of the mountain to a cottage on the far side of the cliff. And there, the sexton could see through the window, lay an old gentile woman, wasting away and sick in her bed. The rabbi swept the floor, chopped the wood, lit the fire, made a large pot of stew, washed the bedclothes and then left quickly in order to get back to the synagogue in time for morning services. The sexton, too, arrived back breathless. "Well," the congregation demanded to know, "Did our rabbi go up to heaven?" The sexton thought for a minute. "Oh, no, my friends," he said and smiled softly. "Our rabbi did not go up to heaven. Our rabbi went much higher than that."

There are some kinds of pain that cannot be taken away in life. Loss. Hurt. Rejection. Disability. But those who enter into the pain of another know what it is to talk about the love of a God who does not change the circumstances that form us but walks through them with us every step of the way.

Pain is that dimension of human life that calls us both to give and to be

45

able to receive the sometimes awkward, often incomplete but always healing care that those who simply sit with those who hurt, forever bring.

The real question, come to think about it, is whether or not the congregation kept their old rabbi or got themselves a new one for the sake of the faith, of course.

To go down into pain with another person breaks open the heart of the God who looks among us always for the face most like God's own.

Response: Name one person who was present to you when you were in pain. Thank them again. Name one person that you were present to when they were in pain. Say a prayer for that person today.

Soul Points

Pray the psalm verse to yourself several times.
Now read the Soul Points by Joan Chittister and respond.

Comfort is a small and tender thing. All it takes is regular presence, patient listening and genuine concern. Maybe that's why there is so little of it in the world. It demands that we go out of ourselves to the other in ways that advantage us not a whit. In fact, comfort is a very expensive thing.

Don't be afraid to let emotional pain into consciousness. That is the only way to identify and heal it. Otherwise it will come out as anger, depression, despair or purposelessness. Embracing the pain, naming it and accepting it, ironically is exactly what takes the teeth out of it.

Comfort is not the useless exercise of trying to talk people out of their pain: "Oh, that's not as bad as you think it is." "You're not really hurting." "Don't worry about it." The fact is that it *is* bad for me. I *do* hurt. I *am* worrying. If you really want to help, simply accept my situation lovingly and ask what you can do to help me through it.

It isn't difficult to survive pain. It is far more difficult to grow beyond it.

"The lowest ebb is the turn of the tide," Henry Wadsworth Longfellow wrote. When something ends without explanation, without warning, without preparation, something new is already on the horizon. Grasp it. There is life.

Response: Choose one Soul Point and write three questions it raises in you.

Photo Prayer

Pray the psalm verse to yourself several times.
Now pray with the photo.

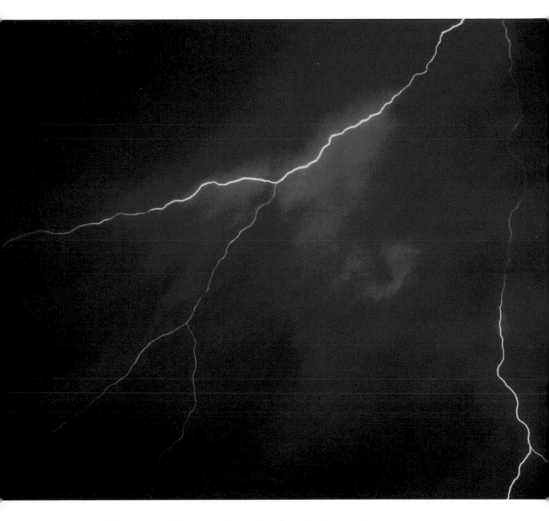

Response: What does this photo have to do with the psalm verse,

Though I walk in the valley of darkness,
no evil do I fear.
Your rod and staff comfort me.

Psalm 23

**Pray the psalm verse to yourself several times.
Now read the story and respond.**

"Will you cure the people who come to you?" the disciple asked the Holy One. "Oh, people don't come to be cured," the Holy One answered. "They come for relief. A cure would require change and that's the last thing in the world they want to do."

Response: What does this story have to do with the psalm,

*Though I walk in the valley of darkness,
no evil do I fear.
Your rod and staff comfort me.*

Psalm 23

Wisdom Notes

Pray the psalm verse to yourself several times.
Now read the Wisdom Notes and respond.

Our prime purpose in this life is to help others.
And, if you cannot help them, at least don't hurt them.
Dalai Lama

Even pain/ Pricks to livelier living.
Amy Lowell

The most massive characters are seared with scars.
E. H. Chapin

Imagine that you are creating a fabric of human destiny
with the object of making men and women happy in the end
but that it is essential and inevitable to torture to death
only one tiny creature and to found that edifice on its unavenged tears;
would you consent to be the architect on those conditions?
Tell me, and tell me the truth.
Fyodor Dostoyevsky

Not to aid one in distress is to kill her or him in your heart.
African proverb

Response: Copy your favorite Wisdom Note. Why did you choose that one?

Personal Reflection

Write the psalm verse from memory.
Say it aloud.

At this point in my life, this psalm verse

Action

Music is often a comfort in times of pain and darkness. Send someone who is in pain and darkness a favorite CD or take them to a concert. Be a "rod and staff" that comforts.

Window Ten

Scripture Reading

Commit your life to God,
and justice will dawn for you.
Your integrity will shine
like the noonday sun.

Psalm 37

Read and memorize the psalm verse.
Pray it over and over again throughout the day
until it comes without effort, until it becomes part of you.

Reflection

Pray the psalm verse to yourself thoughtfully several times.
Now read the Reflection and Response suggestion.

When the man threw his wife down the front steps of the building, the people in the neighborhood explained that he was a good man who had a drinking problem and was out of work and couldn't help himself and she shouldn't nag him. I listened unseen to the adults around me as they shrugged their shoulders and interpreted the world to one another. But even at the age of eleven, I knew they were wrong. He may have been good and out of work and frustrated and sick, but lots of people are. That gave him no right to hurt someone else, to wreak injustice on another, to lose his sense of self. The difference between this situation, I knew, and the situation of the other people on the block who were in equally bad straits, had nothing to do with the circumstances. It had something to do with the way they had learned to approach life to begin with. Something was missing here. What was it?

As the years went by, I began to realize that growing up is not difficult. Maturing is, however. Growth is biological and for all intents and purposes, happens by itself. Maturity, on the other hand, is emotional and takes effort, takes personal commitment.

Maturity implies that something has come to ripe in us. Something is ready. Something is finished developing. Something has become everything of which it is capable. Down deep, in the quiet space inside ourselves, we know that when we're mature, we are not at the mercy of our environment. We respond to life; we don't react to it.

The psalmist names the qualities that constitute maturity: commitment, justice, integrity and spirituality. The mature person lives grounded in God, meets responsibilities, gives the world what is its due and has the kind of self-knowledge that leads to growth till the day we die. Adults do not hurt other people to satisfy their emotional extremes and then make excuses for it.

Response: List three new things you discovered today about yourself, another person, the world. Isn't growth wonderful?

Soul Points

Pray the psalm verse to yourself several times.
Now read the Soul Points by Joan Chittister and respond.

Life is not unique. We all suffer, love, change, strive and die. What is unique is simply the way we each go about it. Some struggle all the way; others, the emotionally adult among us, learn to accept every turn in the road with grace and hope.

☙

To be adult means to be able to take responsibility for the generations both before and after us. It is not adult to make money at the expense of our children's future. It is not adult to take care of ourselves and ignore the needs of those who prepared us to succeed. To be an adult is to pay our debts to the rest of the world.

☙

The adult is the person who is so mindful of their own failings in life that they are eternally gentle with the failings and needs of others.

☙

Integrity demands that the face we present to the world is a valid picture of the intentions and aspirations of our hearts. When we say one thing and live another, think one thing and say another, feel one way and respond another, we have yet to come to full development. We are still two people.

☙

Every stage of life is a learning process. We never ever really get it all together.

Response: Choose one Soul Point and write three questions it raises in you.

Pray the psalm verse to yourself several times.
Now pray with the photo

Response: What does this photo have to do with the psalm verse,

Commit your life to God,
and justice will dawn for you.
Your integrity will shine like the noonday sun.

Psalm 37

Story
**Pray the psalm verse to yourself several times.
Now read the story and respond.**

"When I was ten," the wag wrote on the wall, "I worried about what my parents would think about me."

"When I was twenty, I worried about what my friends would think about me.

"When I was thirty, I worried about what my bosses would think about me.

"When I was forty, I worried about what my neighbors would think about me.

"It wasn't until I got to be fifty that I realized that no one thought about me at all."

Response: What does this story have to do with the psalm,

*Commit your life to God,
and justice will dawn for you.
Your integrity will shine like the noonday sun.*

Psalm 37

Wisdom Notes

Pray the psalm verse to yourself several times.
Now read the Wisdom Notes and respond.

There are years that ask questions and years that answer.
Zona Neale Hurston

Don't try to be a saint. It won't work. Just try to be
a human being. That's harder.
John Dufresene

It is a bit embarrassing
to have been concerned with the human problem all one's life
and find at the end that one has no more to offer by way of advice
than "try to be a little kinder."
Aldous Huxley

You must do the thing you think you cannot do.
Eleanor Roosevelt

The sole meaning of life is to serve humanity.
Leo Tolstoy

Response: Copy your favorite Wisdom Note. Why did you choose that one?

Personal Reflection

Write the psalm verse from memory.
Say it aloud.

At this point in my life, this psalm verse

Action

Name one person you know whose integrity "shines like the noonday sun."
Send that person a card today or call him or her. Tell the person why their
integrity means so much to you.

Window Eleven

Scripture Reading

To you, O God, I lift my soul.
I trust in you…
relieve the distress of my heart.

Psalm 25

Read and memorize the psalm verse.
Pray it over and over again throughout the day
until it comes without effort, until it becomes part of you.

Reflection

Pray the psalm verse to yourself thoughtfully several times.
Now read the Reflection and Response suggestion.

I got a computer when they were still advertising them as "time-savers." Do you notice they don't do that anymore? The truth is that it doesn't take a rocket scientist to figure out that computers don't save time at all. They simply enable us to do things twice as fast as we could without them so that we can now do twice as much in the same amount of time.

The pace of life is getting faster by the day. Everybody wants instant answers to everything. Patience is a spiritual artifact like gargoyles on cathedrals and memorabilia at shrines. The notion of having to wait for something is a thing of the past in the West. Food is fast, communication is instant, human beings are shot through undergrounds and airports, people do six washings a day in machines timed to the minute, money drawn out of bank accounts in one country comes out of holes in the wall on the back streets of small villages in other countries in a matter of seconds. The little things of life, the things we used to take hours and days to do–the cooking, the shopping, the banking, the traveling from point to point, the visiting and human contacts–are speeding up to dizzying proportions. We are pushed from every direction to go faster, to do more, to think less. We rush from birth to death, from place to place, from natural conception to test tube cloning in record time, with little or no opportunity to integrate any of them into our souls, to evaluate them with our minds, to come to grips with the effect of one part of life on us before we are faced with the demands of the next.

The professionals call it "stress." The contemplatives call it a "lack of balance" in life. The social analyst, Alvin Toffler called it "Future Shock," the inability to cope spiritually and psychologically with the increasing effects of technology on our daily lives.

How shall we possibly survive it all without breaking down, without quitting, without rejecting the very things we must most be concerned about in a rapidly changing world if humanity is to remain human at all?

The psalmist is clear: Distress is relieved by right-mindedness. It is not so much how much we do that determines the degree of stress it brings. It is the attitude with which we do it that defines its effect on us. It is the spiritual reserve we bring to natural situations that determine the toll it takes to survive the passing of time gone mad.

Response: List three times when your heart was distressed in the past week. What was it about? Really about? How did you react? However you responded, recite the psalm verse and give it over to God.

Soul Points

Pray the psalm verse to yourself several times.
Now read the Soul Points by Joan Chittister and respond.

Stress strengthens us, it's true, but it also chastens us. We learn that what we survive we do not survive alone.

☞

The problem with stress is that having too little of it leaves us emotional marshmallows, and having too much of it leaves us mentally and physically exhausted. The right amount of stress is whatever it takes to makes us stretch ourselves beyond our comfort zone without leaving us with little or no comfort at all.

☞

A Yugoslav proverb teaches: "What is impossible to change is best to forget." But we don't. Instead we concentrate all our energies on it and wonder how it is that we don't enjoy the rest of life the way we ought to.

☞

"It is well to lie fallow for a while," Martin Tupper wrote. Fallowness, in fact, may be the virtue of the 21st century. Imagine what the grace to glide could bring to a world in a tailspin.

☞

Teresa of Avila prayed: "Let nothing disturb thee,/nothing affright thee;/All things are passing;/God never changeth." People with a spiritual life, psychologists tell us, bear stress better than people for whom God is a question rather than an answer. Who knows? Maybe our stress level is the measure of our spiritual life.

Response: Choose one Soul Point and write three questions it raises in you.

Photo Prayer

Pray the psalm verse to yourself several times.
Now pray with the photo.

To you, O God,
I lift up my soul.
I trust in you...
relieve the distress
of my heart.

Psalm 25

Response: What does this photo have to do with the psalm verse?

**Pray the psalm verse to yourself several times.
Now read the story and respond.**

Once upon a time, two thieves were undergoing trial by ordeal.

If they could walk a wire over the gorge, they would be considered innocent and spared. If, on the other hand, they did not cross the gorge successfully, the belief was that they had been "executed" by the gods for their guilt.

On this particular day, the first thief reached the other side. The second thief, terrified, called to him across the chasm, "How did you do it?"

And the first thief shouted back, "I don't know. All I know is that when I felt myself tottering to one side, I leaned to the other."

Take a lesson: a trusting heart is what enables us to lean to the left when life tilts us to the right. It's called, quite rightly, "balance."

Response: What does this story have to do with the psalm,

To you, O God, I lift up my soul.
I trust in you...
relieve the distress of my heart.

Psalm 25

Wisdom Notes

Pray the psalm verse to yourself several times.
Now read the Wisdom Notes and respond.

Acquire inner peace
and a multitude will find their salvation near you.
St. Seraphim

Calmness is always Godlike.
Ralph Waldo Emerson

The sun will set without thine assistance.
from the Talmud

Time and patience will turn the mulberry leaf into silk.
Eastern proverb

The one whose heart is not content
is like a snake which tries to swallow an elephant.
Chinese proverb

Response: Copy your favorite Wisdom Note. Why did you choose that one?

Personal Reflection

Write the psalm verse from memory.
Say it aloud.

At this point in my life, this Psalm verse

Action

Log your activities, hour by hour, for three days. Then take 30 minutes to read and ponder the log. What did you discover about balance, stress, work and play? If you are not pleased with the results, do something about it. If you are pleased, thank God.

Window Twelve

Scripture Reading

As for us, our days are like grass;
We flower...
the wind blows...
We are gone.

Psalm 103

Read and memorize the psalm verse.
Pray it over and over again throughout the day
until it comes without effort, until it becomes part of you.

Reflection

Pray the psalm verse to yourself thoughtfully several times.
Now read the Reflection and Response suggestion.

The psalmist speaks out of a social situation from which our generation and culture need to learn: to the psalmist life is temporary, fragile, daily "redeemed from the grave." Survival is a matter of massive human effort and natural hardship. The land to be cultivated is desert; water is scarce; foliage is sparse and scrawny and fragile. Every day life is a blessing of mammoth proportions.

But now we take life for granted. We feel invulnerable. Therefore, we lose sight of the brief gift of time and our needs. We know better the needs and weaknesses of others than of our own.

We act as if we're here forever. We spend time as if we have nothing but time. We fritter away the great things of life: gospel commitments, family, prayer, nature, responsibility for play and things that serve ourselves–ambition, clothes, consumption, play.

We think we have forever. We'll do what we have to do later: we'll reconcile "later;" we'll settle down "later;" we'll pray "later;" we'll get some order in our lives "later;" we'll study the nuclear thing, the economic thing, the racism thing, the sexism thing, "later." After we get finished with the very important things we're doing now.

Nevertheless, today we too have been "redeemed from the grave." The question is "Why?" Whatever the reason: do it now.

Response: Complete this sentence, In every life there should be....
Do you have it? What is it that you want most in life right now and have least time for? What are you choosing instead? Why? Look at that very closely. It's telling you something you need to attend to.

Soul Points

Pray the psalm verse to yourself several times.
Now read the Soul Points by Joan Chittister and respond.

It is a paltry life indeed that centers only on itself. Think for a moment how you have spent your time. If you died tomorrow, who besides yourself would notice? Whose life besides your own would lose something? If you can't name two hands' worth of people, maybe you ought to give some thought to joining a service organization and volunteering your time.

☞

We are the only hands God has. Creation goes on creating through us. What are you doing for the world at this time in your life that God wants done?

☞

The psalmist reminds us that however long life is, it's still far too short to waste. But what precisely does it mean to "waste" time? The Puritans would say that we are wasting time when we are not engaged in some kind of useful work. Americans would say that it's a period when we're not moving toward a given goal. The hedonist would say that it's when we're not enjoying ourselves. The psalmist would say that it's a period in which we fail to live life fully, to be aware of it and its meaning for us at a given moment. Which one are you living? Is it good for you?

☞

Time is meant to free us for life but instead time enslaves us. Instead of listening to the people we're with, we keep checking our watches to make sure that we're on time for the person who's coming next. We live with our minds on something else instead of the presence of God in the present. So we miss our children growing up. We miss the middle years of marriage. We miss the calls within us to live life in new ways. We lose time and think we're living. How sad. Be here now.

☞

Filling time is not always the way to use time best. Sometimes we learn a great deal more by just sitting and thinking about it, looking at it and taking stock of it, comparing our lives with the lives of those around us. This life is the only one we have. What a pity to come to the end of it saying, "I could have... I should have...but I didn't."

Response: Choose one Soul Point and write three questions it raises in you.

Photo Prayer

Pray the psalm verse to yourself several times.
Now pray with the photo.

Response: What does this photo have to do with the psalm verse,

As for us, our days are like grass;
We flower...
the wind blows...
We are gone.

Psalm 103

Story

**Pray the psalm verse to yourself several times.
Now read the story and respond.**

I had just one desire—to give myself completely to God. So I headed for the monastery. An old monk asked me, "What is it you want?" I said, "I just want to give myself to God." I expected him to be gentle, fatherly, but he shouted at me. NOW!

I was stunned. He shouted again, "NOW!" Then he reached for a club and came after me. I turned and ran. He kept coming after me, brandishing his club and shouting, "NOW, NOW."

That was years ago. He still follows me, wherever I go. Always that stick, always that "NOW!"

Theophane the Monk, *Tales of a Magic Monastery*

Response: What does this story have to do with the psalm,

As for us, our days are like grass;
We flower...
the wind blows...
We are gone.

Psalm 103

Wisdom Notes

Pray the psalm verse to yourself several times.
Now read the Wisdom Notes and respond.

We will go before God to be judged, and God will ask us,
"Where are your wounds?" And we will say, "We have no wounds."
And God will ask, "Was there nothing worth fighting for?"
Rev. Allan Beosak

Destiny is no matter of chance. It is a matter of choice.
It is not a thing to be waited for, it is a thing to be achieved.
William Jennings Bryan

Life is not lost by dying;
life is lost minute by minute, day by dragging day,
in all the thousand small uncaring ways.
Stephen Vincent Benét

Time is the only coin of your life.
It is the only coin you have,
and only you can determine how it will be spent.
Carl Sandburg

The opera ain't over until the fat lady sings.
Author Unknown

Response: Copy your favorite Wisdom Note. Why did you choose that one?

Personal Reflection

Write the psalm verse from memory.
Say it aloud.

At this point in my life, this psalm verse

Action

Do at least one thing you really like every single day. Do you like to be alone?
Say so and do it. Do you like to read or play the piano or paint? Say so and do
it. Do you like to spend time with friends? Call them up. Plan it. Don't simply
let "all your days pass away...."

Window Thirteen

Scripture Reading

When God brought Israel back to Zion,
it seemed like a dream.
Then our mouths were filled with laughter;
on our lips there were songs of joy.

Psalm 126

Read and memorize the psalm verse.
Pray it over and over again throughout the day
until it comes without effort, until it becomes part of you.

Reflection

Pray the psalm verse to yourself thoughtfully several times.
Now read the Reflection and Response suggestion.

This month's psalm talks to us about laughing, a too-often overlooked spiritual discipline. The important thing to realize about this psalm is that it takes place after the destruction of Jerusalem and the Babylonian captivity. These people had suffered mightily. But in their freedom they did not become bitter. They learned to laugh–and so must we.

The function of humor is not to make light of serious things. The function of a good story is to enable us to see life differently than we ordinarily do, to topple the mighty from their thrones so that all of us become equal again.

Humor gives spirit to a people when they have no other defense. Jews delighted, for instance, in telling the story of the old man in top hat and phylacteries who appeared at the local Gestapo station. He was holding an ad in his hand that called for young, healthy Aryans to promise service for the Führer. "What are you doing here?" the commandant asked the old Jew. "I'm answering this ad," the old man said. "What?" the commandant asked incredulously. "That's ridiculous. You're not young." "No," the old man said, "I'm 73." "And you're certainly not Aryan." "No," the old man said, "I'm Jewish–both sides." "And you're obviously not committed to serving the Führer." "No," the old man said, "I wouldn't do a single thing for that man." "Then why are you here?" the commandant insisted angrily. "Vell," the old Jew said, "I just came down to tell you that on me you shouldn't count."

Point: Humor gives a people dignity in situations that denigrate them. Laughter gives us relief from the burden of dailiness. No amount of coercion can break an unbreakable spirit humor teaches us. And someday that cagey old man, buried deep in our spirits, becomes the patron saint of our own silent, laughing resistance to systems that reject us but cannot survive our disdain. Humor cuts oppressors down to size, takes their sting away, renders them powerless to destroy us. Don't give in to what diminishes you. Learn to laugh at it and reduce its power over you.

Response: Here's a good idea, This week when you're really upset about the important things in life—like being late for an appointment, or watching your dog knock over your best vase, or finding out that the car won't start, or discovering that the screwdriver isn't where it's supposed to be—laugh. The problem will disappear because nothing is a problem unless we call it that.

Soul Points

Pray the psalm verse to yourself several times.
Now read the Soul Points by Joan Chittister and respond.

My God is a God who laughs. And why not? Here we are—racing through life assuming that everything depends on us. And nothing is perfect yet. Wouldn't you think we would get used to imperfection. No wonder God finds us so funny. Well, better that than unbearable.

☞

Never confuse humor and ridicule. Humor cleanses the soul of tension; ridicule creates tension. It makes a person the butt of public derision and takes joy out of life. It hurts. When we laugh at what is not a mere lapse of the normal, not changeable, not the triumph of innocence over pomp, that is not humor. To laugh at physical defects, at ethnic characteristics, at human effort is not funny. That is laughter become a weapon.

☞

The thing about laughter is you have to take it seriously. That, or end up a shriveled up excuse for half a person. Those who laugh, last.

☞

"In this world there are only two tragedies," Oscar Wilde wrote. "One is not getting what you want; the other is getting it." Isn't it the truth? Learn to laugh. It's a survival mechanism.

☞

"My doctor gave me six months to live, but when I couldn't pay the bill he gave me six months more," Walter Matthau said. See what I mean? Just thinking the unthinkable makes us feel better in a minute.

Response: Choose one Soul Point and write three questions it raises in you.

Photo Prayer

Pray the psalm verse to yourself several times.
Now pray with the photo.

When God brought Israel
back to Zion,
it seemed like a dream.
Then our mouths
were filled with laughter;
on our lips
there were songs of joy.

Psalm 126

Response: What does this photo have to do with the psalm verse.

**Pray the psalm verse to yourself several times.
Now read the story and respond.**

Of the great Zen Master Rinzai it was said that each night the last thing he did before he went to bed was let out a great big belly laugh that resounded through the corridors and was heard in every building of the monastery grounds.

And the first thing he did when he woke at dawn was burst into peals of laughter so loud they woke up every monk, no matter how deep his slumber.

His disciples asked him repeatedly to tell them why he laughed, but he wouldn't. And when he died he carried the secret of his laughter with him to the grave.

- from *Taking Flight*, Anthony de Mello, S.J.

Response: What does this story have to do with the psalm,

*When God brought Israel back to Zion,
it seemed like a dream.
Then our mouths were filled with laughter;
on our lips there were songs of joy.*

Psalm 126

Wisdom Notes

Pray the psalm verse to yourself several times.
Now read the Wisdom Notes and respond.

They deserve paradise who make their companions laugh.
The Koran

The most wasted day of all is that on which we have not laughed.
Nicholas Chamfort

One can never speak enough
of the virtues, the dangers, the power of shared laughter.
Francoise Sagan

Nobody ever died of laughter.
Max Beerbohm

Among those whom I like or admire, I can find no common denominator,
but among those whom I love, I can: all of them make me laugh.
Auden

Response: Copy your favorite Wisdom Note. Why did you choose that one?

Personal Reflection

Write the psalm verse from memory.
Say it aloud.

At this point in my life, this psalm verse

Action

Go rent a movie that makes you laugh, one that "fills your mouth with laughter, puts songs of joy on your lips." Watch it with some friends. Don't forget to make popcorn.

Window Fourteen

Scripture Reading

What else have I in heaven but you?
Apart from you I want nothing on earth.
My heart leaps for joy
for you, O God, are my portion forever.

Psalm 73

Read and memorize the psalm verse.
Pray it over and over again throughout the day
until it comes without effort, until it becomes part of you.

Reflection

Pray the psalm verse to yourself thoughtfully several times.
Now read the Reflection and Response suggestion.

It's not easy to write about simplicity in a complex world. It is even harder to think about it. The concept seems to evoke one of two reactions: guilt "I know I have too much, but I don't have a clue how else to live?"or ridicule "I know I can't have everything. Wherever would I put it?" The fact is that frugality is cheap simplicity. Simplicity requires a great deal more from us than simply getting rid of the gadgets we don't want or the surplus we don't need. Simplicity requires that we learn how to live a centered life, to "make God our portion," in a world that tears our days, our lives, our psyches into tangled shreds.

Isn't simplicity really what the ancients called "purity of heart" that singleminded search for the essence of life rather than for a grasping after its frills?

Simplicity is openness to the beauty of the present, whatever its shape, whatever its lack. Simplicity, clearly, leads to freedom of soul. When we cultivate a sense of "enoughness," when we learn to enjoy things for their own sakes, when we learn to be gentle even with what is lacking in ourselves, we find ourselves free to be where we are and to stop mourning where we are not.

Simplicity of life in a complex and complicated world is marked, I think, by four characteristics: a life is simple if it is honest; if it is unencumbered;

if it is open to the ideas of others; if it is serene in the midst of a mindless momentum that verges on the chaotic. And which of these do you do best? And which of these do you do least?

Response: List ten things you feel that you cannot live without. Comment on that list.

Soul Points

Pray the psalm verse to yourself several times.
Now read the Soul Points by Joan Chittister and respond.

Simplicity of life is what the poet-president Sister Madeleva Wolff, CSC, called "the habitually relaxed grasp." It isn't what we have accumulated, in other words, that measures the simplicity of our lives, it's what we're willing to let go of when we must, when we should.

☞

It's when we set out to shape every element of life to our own designs that we lose all sense of simplicity. "Going with the flow" is a very liberating spiritual discipline that is good for interpersonal relationships, social life and ulcers.

☞

Pretending to be something we are not, a little bit better placed, a touch more educated than we really are, a family of more means than we actually have, puts us in a position of eternal jeopardy. Someone will surely find out. Wouldn't it be less tension-producing, let alone a demonstration of holy simplicity, just to be honest about it all?

☞

When people with rigid dietary fancies put other people under a great deal of strain cooking for them, I can't help but wonder how really simple that is. When people handle their own schedules very well because they simply refuse to have their personal priorities interrupted by anybody else's needs, is that living "the simple life?" Everybody else is forced to bend to suit the demand so everybody else's lives wind up more and more intricate, involved, difficult as a result. So who is really practicing simplicity of life in these cases? Simplicity, I am convinced, is far more than having life on our own terms whatever its effect on others.

☞

The simple person pays close attention to the agitations that eat at the heart. It is our agitations that tell us where life has gone astray for us, has become unbearably complex and eternally confused.

Response: Choose one Soul Point and write three questions that it raises in you.

Pray
the psalm verse
to yourself
several times.
Now pray
with the photo.

What else have I in heaven but you?
Apart from you I want nothing on earth.
My heart leaps for joy
for you, O God, are my portion forever.

Psalm 73

Response:
What does
this photo
have to do
with the
psalm verse?

Pray the psalm verse to yourself several times.
Now read the story and respond.

Ryokan, a Zen master, lived the simplest kind of life in a little hut at the foot of the mountain. One evening a thief visited the hut only to discover that there was nothing there to steal.

Ryokan returned and discovered him in the act. "You have come a long way to visit me," he told the prowler, "and you should not return empty-handed. Please take my clothes as a gift."

The thief was bewildered. He took the clothes and slunk away.

"Poor fellow," Ryokan mused, "I wish I could give him the beautiful moon."

Response: What does this story have to do with the psalm,

What else have I in heaven but you?
Apart from you
I want nothing on earth.
My heart leaps for joy
for you, O God,
are my portion forever.

Psalm 73

Wisdom Notes

Pray the psalm verse to yourself several times.
Now read the Wisdom Notes and respond.

We only own what cannot be lost in a shipwreck.
Arab proverb

Seek God and not where God lives.
Desert Fathers and Mothers

To be without some of the things you want
is an indispensable part of happiness.
Bertrand Russell

Manifest plainness,
Embrace simplicity,
Reduce selfishness,
Have few desires.
Lao-Tzu

Our life is frittered away by detail.
Simplify, simplify, simplify.
Henry David Thoreau

Response: Copy your favorite Wisdom Note. Why did you choose that one?

Personal Reflection

Write the Scripture psalm from memory.
Say it aloud.

At this point in my life, this psalm verse

Action

Today give away three things: one item that is of no use to you, one item that you treasure and one item that you just bought.

Window Fifteen

Scripture Reading

You love those who search for truth.
In wisdom, center me,
for you know my frailty.

Psalm 51

Read and memorize the psalm verse.
Pray it over and over again throughout the day
until it comes without effort, until it becomes part of you.

Reflection

Pray the psalm verse to yourself thoughtfully several times.
Now read the Reflection and Response suggestion.

The dictum "Know thyself," which appeared on the statue of the Oracle of Apollo at Delphi in sixth century B.C. Greece, is one of the oldest directives in Western philosophy. It's good advice. We so often project onto other people the tendencies we fail to recognize in ourselves. In our time, however, the concern is as much about self-esteem as it is about self-knowledge. Both positions are valuable. But both of them are insufficient, I think.

Self-knowledge gives us perspective and self-esteem gives us confidence, but it's self-acceptance that gives us peace of heart. It implies, of course, that I know myself and value myself. Yet, unless I can simply start by accepting myself, it is possible that neither of the other two dimensions can ever come to life in me. Clearly, even if I know who I am, even if I admit the truth about myself, if I don't accept what I see there, I can never really value it. Worse, I'll live in fear that someone else will see to the core of me and reject me, too.

But, the psalmist teaches us, that's precisely where the God who birthed us, our loving Mother God, becomes the mainstay, not the menace of our lives. God knows exactly who we are. God knows our frailty. And God accepts it. And gathers it in. God loves us, not despite it, but because of it, because of the effort it implies and the trust it demands. There is glory in the clay of us. There is beauty in becoming. The static notion of life, the idea that we can become something and stay that way, is a false one. We face newness all our lives. We search all our days for truth. And God loves us for the seeking. What we need is not perfection. What we need is a center that stabilizes us in times of change, in us as well as around us.

Response: Think a minute, What are the two deepest desires of your soul for yourself? What's keeping you from attaining them?

Soul Points

Pray the psalm verse to yourself several times.
Now read the Soul Points by Joan Chittister and respond.

"In wisdom, center me," the psalmist has us pray. Everybody is centered in something. In each of us there is that internal magnet that guides our decisions and occupies our thoughts. For some it's fear, for others it's ambition, for many it's social acceptance, for a portion of humanity it's independence, for real unfortunates it's perfection of one kind or another. When the internal lodestone is wisdom, however, we are able to take life as it is and just be happy that we learned from it instead of being crushed by it.

Anyone who says they want to be young again is either a fool or a liar. In the first place, that period was no easier than this one. Oftentimes harder, in fact. In the second place, the task of that time was to bring us to this one. There is something in the now for us that will make the future even better if we can just keep moving toward it. Don't stop living just because life isn't perfect.

I write my life in my own blood. Anything else is sham. When I hurt, I'll know what hurt is all about. When I fail, I'll find out what survival is all about. When I love, I'll come to know what selflessness is all about. And when we know those things, we will be both wise and fully alive.

Self-acceptance is not self-satisfaction. It is self-realization. It is the ability to see ourselves as we are and to take that as the raw material out of which we build a wonderful life. Our life, not someone else's. I don't have to be a concert pianist to play at parties. All I have to do is to love being the one who is able to play at parties.

Wisdom is what's left over after the experience has ended.

Response: Choose one Soul Point and write three questions it raises in you.

Photo Prayer

Pray the psalm verse to yourself several times.
Now pray with the photo.

Response: What does this photo have to do with the psalm verse,

You love those who search for truth.
In wisdom, center me,
for you know my frailty.

Psalm 51

Story
**Pray the psalm verse to yourself several times.
Now read the story and respond.**

I was a neurotic for years. I was anxious and depressed and selfish. And everyone kept telling me to change. And everyone kept telling me how neurotic I was. And I resented them, and I agreed with them, and I wanted to change, but I just couldn't bring myself to change, no matter how hard I tried.

What hurt the most was that my best friend also kept telling me how neurotic I was. He too kept insisting that I change. And I agreed with him too, though I couldn't bring myself to resent him. And I felt so powerless and so trapped.

Then one day he said to me, "Don't change. Stay as you are. It really doesn't matter whether you change or not. I love you just as you are; I cannot help loving you."

These words sounded like music to my ears: "Don't change. Don't change. Don't change. I love you."

And I relaxed. And I came alive. And, oh wondrous marvel, I changed.

- from *The Song of the Bird*, Anthony De Mello, S.J.

Response: What does this story have to do with the psalm,

*You love those who search for truth.
In wisdom, center me,
for you know my frailty.*

Psalm 51

Wisdom Notes

Pray the psalm verse to yourself several times.
Now read the Wisdom Notes and respond.

Life is full of internal dramas, instantaneous and sensational,
played to an audience of one.
Anthony Pail

It is good to have an end to journey towards,
but it is the journey that matters in the end.
Ursula Le Guin

Rose is a rose is a rose is a rose, is a rose.
Gertrude Stein

I'm the greatest.
Muhammad Ali

The image of myself which I try to create in my own mind
in order that I may love myself is very different from the image
which I try to create in the minds of others in order that they may love me.
W.H. Auden

If you wish to live, you must first attend your own funeral.
Katherine Mansfield

Response: Copy your favorite Wisdom Note. Why did you choose that one?

Personal Reflection

Write the psalm verse from memory.
Say it aloud.

At this point in my life, this psalm verse

_____

Action

Stand in front of a mirror today and smile. Then repeat the psalm verse five times: "You love those who search for truth. In wisdom, center me, for you know my frailty."

Window Sixteen

Scripture Reading

I am like an olive tree,
growing in the house of God.

Psalm 52

Read and memorize the psalm verse.
Pray it over and over again throughout the day
until it comes without effort, until it becomes part of you.

Reflection

Pray the psalm verse to yourself thoughtfully several times.
Now read the Reflection and Response suggestion.

Life is not about going through the motions from birth to death. Life is about the development of self to the point of unbridled joy. Life is about trusting our talents and following our gifts. But how? Olive trees hint at the answer even today.

Olive trees are a very important and very meaningful image in Jewish literature. To the Jewish mind, to grow like "an olive tree" is no small thing. It isn't easy to grow trees in the Middle East. Sand is hardly a conducive environment for forestry. Yet, there is one wood that seems to thrive on the difficulty of the process. There is one tree with a natural talent for life in the middle of nowhere. The olive tree grows hard wood on barren ground, with little water, for a long, long time.

To "grow like an olive tree," then, means to grow without much help, to grow hardy, to grow long and to grow on very little nourishment. The olive tree doesn't need much to develop, it gives good wood at the end of a long, slow process of growth, and it doesn't die easily, sometimes not for thousands of years. The olive tree has a talent for life. There are some olive trees in the Garden of Olives, in fact, that scholars estimate were there the night of the Last Supper when Christ went there to pray. Startling, isn't it?

In this culture, in this age, on the other hand, the temptation is to think that everything–including our own natural abilities–ought to come easily. We want fast service and quick results. We want a lot for nothing. We want the greatest degree of return for the least amount of effort. And we want out of whatever doesn't work the first time. There is very little of the focused, the hardy, the persistent olive tree in us. There is very little talent for talent in us.

Yet talents that lie dormant in our souls destroy us from the inside out. If we do not learn to slowly, patiently, painfully, if necessary, let them come to life in us, we risk our own robotization.

We give ourselves over to the pain of a living death. Talent is the gift that will not go away.

Response: Talent is the unexpressed part of me, the part I'm dying to try and fear to attempt. "At my age?" we say. "In my position?" "With my responsibilities?" Well, do you want to die happy? Then, go ahead, try it.

Soul Points

Pray the psalm verse to yourself several times.
Now read the Soul Points by Joan Chittister and respond.

To have a talent for gardening and not to develop it is to deprive the world of color. Imagine how gray the world would be if all the gardeners of the world never took flower growing seriously. The question is, of what are we depriving the world?

Talent without the perseverance necessary to develop it is cheap. Too many people spend their lives talking about what they might have done if they had only stayed at something long enough for it to bear fruit.

Talent is to be used for its highest possible purpose, to be a flash of light in a world that needs to see just one more foot ahead of itself.

Vladimir Nabokov wrote with great insight, "Genius is an African who dreams up snow." Genius, in other words, always does the undoable. Don't be afraid of the new ideas that come from strange places. Sift every one of them carefully but sift them all with the hope that comes from searching for diamonds in white sand.

If you are reading these reflections with sadness because of all the things in life you always wanted to do but never did, you have missed the point. "It is never too late to be what you might have been," George Eliot said. Talent is that unsatisfied part of us that is dying to be developed and which, until it is, will lurk within us agitating and waiting to be recognized. If not by the world, at least by you. Go out this week and get whatever it is–the brushes, the chisels, the books, the camera, the kit, the lessons–that you need to begin what you have always wanted to do. Grandma Moses began to paint in her eighties. And so, come to think of it, did my aunt.

Response: Choose one Soul Point and write three questions it raises in you.

Photo Prayer

Pray
the psalm verse
to yourself
several times.
Now pray
with the photo.

*I am
like an olive tree,
growing in the house
of God.*

Psalm 52

Response:
What does
this photo
have to do
with the
psalm verse?

**Pray the psalm verse to yourself several times.
Now read the story and respond.**

A writer arrived at the monastery to write a book about the Enlightened One.

"People say you are a genius. Are you?" the writer asked.

"You might say so," said the Enlightened One.

The writer continued, "And what makes one a genius?"

"The ability to recognize," answered the Enlightened One.

"Recognize what?" the writer asked.

"A genius," the Enlightened One said, "is one who can recognize the butterfly in a caterpillar; the eagle in an egg; the saint in a selfish human being."

Response: What does this story have to do with the psalm,

*I am like an olive tree,
growing in the house of God.*

Psalm 52

Wisdom Notes

Pray the psalm verse to yourself several times.
Now read the Wisdom Notes and respond.

The absence of risk is a sure sign of mediocrity.
Charles de Foucauld

In the long run we hit only what we aim at.
David Thoreau

Not a day passes over the earth, but men and women of no note
do great deeds, speak great words and suffer noble sorrows.
Charles Reade

Consider the postage stamp.
Its usefulness consists in the ability to stick to one thing until it gets there.
Josh Billings

The principal mark of genius is not perfection
but originality, the opening of new frontiers.
Arthur Koestler.

Response: Copy your favorite Wisdom Note. Why did you choose that one?

Personal Reflection

Write the psalm verse from memory.
Say it aloud.

At this point in my life, this psalm verse

Action

"Follow your bliss," Joseph Campbell wrote, "and you'll never work another day in your life." What do you find blissful? That is probably your talent. Today "follow your bliss."

Window Seventeen

Scripture Reading

*I kept my sin secret
and my frame wasted away.
Day and night
your hand was heavy upon me.*

Psalm 32

**Read and memorize the psalm verse.
Pray it over and over again throughout the day
until it comes without effort, until it becomes part of you.**

Reflection

**Pray the psalm verse to yourself thoughtfully several times.
Now read the Reflection and Response suggestion.**

This psalm is a piece of very good psychology about the burdens we carry within us, our unforgiven sins.

When we don't face our faults, our problems, our weakness, our angers, our sense of inadequacy, worse, when we blame them on others, or deny them, or need to be perfect, or become defensive, we refuse to accept ourselves. Every doctor and psychologist in the country sees the effect of that in their offices every day.

We all have things we need to forgive in ourselves or face in ourselves. We have things we know we ought to ask forgiveness for from someone else but pride and stubbornness hold us back.

These things become a barrier between us and the community, a hot stone in the pit of the stomach, a block to real happiness. And nothing is going to get better until we face them.

Forgiveness occurs when we don't need to hold a grudge anymore: When we are strong enough to be independent of whatever, whoever it was that so ruthlessly uncovered the need in us. Forgiveness is not the problem; it's living till it comes that taxes all the strength we have.

Some people think that forgiveness is incomplete until things are just as they were before. But the truth is that after great hurt, things are never what they were before: they can only be better or nothing at all. Both of which are acceptable states of life.

"Life is an adventure in forgiveness," Norman Cousins said. You will, in other words, have lots of opportunity to practice. Don't wait too long to start or life will have gone by before you ever lived it.

Response: When someone apologizes to you, say, "Thanks so much for being concerned. Don't give it another thought." (Feels good, doesn't it? That's what God is like.)

Soul Points

Pray the psalm verse to yourself several times.
Now read the Soul Points by Joan Chittister and respond.

Those who have cultivated humility and self-criticism know the pain of failing themselves and so can rise to even greater heights because their tears have made them whole.

☙

Don't confuse weakness with sin. Most of us struggle with something we can never quite conquer. It is precisely that struggle that can become the stuff of compassion with others.

☙

The value of sin is to learn forgiveness: how to get it and how to give it, as well.

☙

People who have never faced their own sins are people who have yet to know themselves. But without self-knowledge, real spiritual development is impossible.

☙

The inability to forgive another almost certainly arises out of an inability to forgive ourselves. When we refuse to give ourselves permission to be anything but perfect–as if failure did not bring its own lessons in life–we certainly are not able to forgive anyone else.

Response: Choose one Soul Point and write three questions it raises in you.

Photo Prayer

Pray the psalm verse
to yourself several times.
Now pray with the photo.

*I kept my sin secret
and my frame
wasted away.
Day and night
your hand
was heavy upon me.*

Psalm 32

Response: What does this photo have to do with the psalm verse.

Story

Pray the psalm verse to yourself several times.
Now read the story and respond.

Once a brother committed a sin in Scetis, and the elders assembled and sent for Abbot Moses.

He, however, did not want to go.

Then the priest sent a message to him saying: "Come, everybody is waiting for you."

So he finally got up to go. And he took a worn-out basket with holes, filled it with sand, and carried it along.

The people who came to meet him said: "What is this, Father?"

Then the old man said: "My sins are running out behind me, yet I do not see them. And today I have come to judge the sins of someone else."

When they heard this, they said nothing to the brother, and pardoned him.

Tales of the Desert Fathers and Mothers

Response: What does this story have to do with the psalm,

I kept my sin secret
and my frame wasted away.
Day and night your hand
was heavy upon me.

Psalm 32

Wisdom Notes

Pray the psalm verse to yourself several times.
Now read the Wisdom Notes and respond.

The saints are sinners who keep on trying.
Robert Louis Stevenson

Sin cannot be undone, only forgiven.
Igor Stravinsky

What God gave Adam was not forgiveness from sin.
What God gave Adam was the right to begin again.
Elie Wiesel

It is often the most wicked who know the nearest path to the shrine.
Japanese proverb

Forgiveness is the key to action and freedom.
Hannah Arendt

Response: Copy your favorite Wisdom Note. Why did you choose that one?

Personal Reflection

Write the psalm verse from memory.
Say it aloud.

At this point in my life, this psalm verse

_____

Action

You've heard of Random Acts of Kindness? Today perform a Random Act of Forgiveness. You choose. Whom haven't you spoken to in years, months, weeks? Send them a card. Call them. Or maybe you have to forgive yourself for something. Give it a try.

Window Eighteen

Scripture Reading

My soul waits for you;
I count on your word.

Psalm 130

Read and memorize the psalm verse.
Pray it over and over again throughout the day
until it comes without effort, until it becomes part of you.

Reflection

Pray the psalm verse to yourself thoughtfully several times.
Now read the Reflection and Response suggestion.

Commitment and enthusiasm are two concepts that are, unfortunately, often confused.

Commitment is that quality of life that depends more on the ability to wait for something to come to fulfillment–through good days and through bad–than it does on being able to sustain an emotional extreme for it over a long period of time. Enthusiasm is excitement fed by satisfaction.

The tangle of the two ideas, however, is exactly what leads so many people to fall off in the middle of a project. When the work ceases to feel good, when praying for peace gets nowhere, when the marriage counseling fails to reinvigorate the marriage, when the projects and the plans and the hopes worse than fail, they fizzle, that's when the commitment really starts. When enthusiasm wanes, and romantic love dies and moral apathy–a debilitating loss of purpose and energy–sets in, that is the point at which we are asked to give as much as we get. That's when what we thought was an adventure turns into a commitment. Sometimes a long, hard, demanding one that tempts us to despair. As if God will ever abandon the good. As if waiting for God's good time were a waste of our time. As if God's Word of love will ever fail us in the end. Once upon a time, the dove said to the cloud, "How many snowflakes does it take to break a branch?" "I have no idea," the cloud replied. "I simply keep on snowing until it does." "Mmmmm," the little dove mused. "I wonder how many voices it will take before peace comes?"

Commitment is that quality of human nature that tells us not to count days or months or years, conversations or efforts or rejections, but simply to go on going on until "all things are in the fullness of time," until everything is ready, until all hearts are in waiting for the Word of God in this situation to be fulfilled.

When we feel most discouraged, most fatigued, most alone is precisely the time we must not quit.

Response: Most of the problems on earth are solvable. The problem is not that we don't have the technological skill. The problem is that we don't have the political will. Which translated means that you and I don't really care enough yet to demand a solution. Name three things to which you are committed. Name one thing you did this year to make them happen.

Soul Points

Pray the psalm verse to yourself several times.
Now read the Soul Points by Joan Chittister and respond.

"The greatest thing of all is caring," Frederich Von Hugel wrote. "Caring is everything." And he should know. Von Hugel, the lay theologian whose work helped to usher in the era of modern theology and Scripture study, knew resistance on every side from the church he loved. Nevertheless, he persisted and his legacy lives on in us. By the way, even in the face of all that pressure, these were the last words he said. On his deathbed. Now that's commitment.

☞

How do you know when you're really committed to something? Easy. When what happens to it still affects you, you are committed to it, whatever the discomfort of it all.

☞

Apathy, indifference, listlessness are often simply the countersigns of adulthood. Children wait for someone else to satisfy them. Adults are people who are able to make their own happiness. To find nothing in anything is often because we put nothing into everything.

☞

Mae West said once, "Too much of a good thing is wonderful." How freeing. Commitment, that insight implies, is the ability to go overboard for something. If you're not unbalanced about something in life, you haven't begun to live.

☞

Commitment and masochism are not synonyms. Sometimes commitment to the Word of God demands that we leave what we have already begun so that real life can come to fullness in us.

☞

The psychiatrist Rollo May teaches that hate is not the opposite of love; apathy is. What we hate is at least still worth enough to us to arouse in us an intense human response.

Response: Choose one Soul Point and write three questions it raises in you.

Photo Prayer

Pray the psalm verse to yourself several times.
Now pray with the photo.

My soul waits for you;
I count on your word.

Psalm 130

Response: What does this photo have to do with the psalm verse?

Story
**Pray the psalm verse to yourself several times.
Now read the story and respond.**

A Zen monk in Japan wanted to publish the holy books, which at that time were available only in Chinese. The books were to be printed with wood blocks in an edition of seven thousand copies, a tremendous undertaking.

The monk began by traveling and collecting donations for this purpose. A few sympathizers would give him a hundred pieces of gold, but most of the time he received only small coins. After ten years, the monk had enough money to begin his task.

But then there was a terrible flood in the area and famine followed. So the monk took the funds he had collected for the books and spent them to save others from starving. Then he began his work of collecting again.

Fifteen years later an epidemic spread over the country. To help his people, the monk again gave away what he had collected.

For a third time he started his work, and after twenty years his wish was fulfilled—the books were printed. The printing blocks which produced the first edition of the holy books can be seen today in a monastery in Kyoto.

The Japanese, however, tell their children that the monk really made three sets of holy books. And, they explain with great pride, the first two invisible sets surpass even the third.

Response: What does this story have to do with the psalm,

My soul waits for you;
I count on your word.

Psalm 130

Wisdom Notes

Pray the psalm verse to yourself several times.
Now read the Wisdom Notes and respond.

Science may have found a cure for most evils,
but it has found no remedy for the worst of them all—
the apathy of human beings.
Helen Keller

The hottest places in hell are reserved for those who,
in time of great moral crisis, maintain their neutrality.
Dante

Never doubt that a small group of thoughtful, committed citizens
can change the world; indeed, it's the only thing that ever has.
Margaret Mead

The irony of commitment is that it is deeply liberating—
in work, in play, in love.
Anne Morriss

If you stand for something important,
write it in big bold letters so that someone can see it.
Socrates.

Response: Copy your favorite Wisdom Note. Why did you choose that one?

Personal Reflection

Write the psalm verse from memory.
Say it aloud.

At this point in my life, this psalm verse

Action

It takes effort to keep the passion of commitment burning. Try rekindling the passion in one commitment that may have waned in your life: a promise, a personal relationship, a cause of justice or peace, the spreading of the Gospel. Take one action today to try and rekindle the flame.

94

Window Nineteen

Scripture Reading

*Be still
and know that I am God.*

Psalm 46

Read and memorize the psalm verse.
Pray it over and over again throughout the day
until it comes without effort, until it becomes part of you.

Reflection

Pray the psalm verse to yourself thoughtfully several times.
Now read the Reflection and Response suggestion.

Two images surround this theme of Sabbath and leisure for me. The first memory lies buried in old poetry, the second in a rabbi whose name I cannot remember.

The first incident happened during my first year of high school, I think. I had somehow stumbled on the works of the French poet Charles Peguy who wrote, "I love the one who sleeps, says God." The words didn't mean much to me at the time; if anything they seemed a little silly, or at very least, confusing. But, interestingly enough, those words have stayed with me every year since. Now, decades of monastic life later, I have come to understand the wisdom of them, I have begun to realize their importance. Sleep, I now understand, is a sign of trust. The ability to rest gives the world back to God for a while. Rest, Sabbath, leisure all release a part of us that the corsets of time and responsibility every day seek to smother and try to suppress.

The second incident happened during a trip to Jerusalem years later. A local rabbi had joined us for the meal that celebrated the opening of Shabbat. I remember, for obvious reasons, as if it were yesterday, his final example of the perfect Sabbath observance. "You see this?" he said, taking a pen out of his breast pocket and twirling it in his fingers. "I am a writer and on the Sabbath I never allow myself to carry a pen. On the Sabbath I must allow myself to become new again."

In those two moments, I discovered what the psalmist tries to teach us in Psalm 46 about learning to be still. It is more than the simple observation that everyone needs to let go a little, to get rested enough to work harder next week, to change pace from the hectic to the chaotic. It is far beyond the fact that everyone needs a vacation. Oh no, it is much more than that. What this month's psalm verse teaches us is the simple truth that a soul without a sense of Sabbath is an agitated soul.

Response: To become something new we must consciously do something different than we have been doing before this. Try it next Sunday. See if Monday is a better experience because of it.

Soul Points

Pray the psalm verse to yourself several times.
Now read the Soul Points by Joan Chittister and respond.

The first reason for the Sabbath, the rabbis teach, is to equalize the rich and the poor. Safe from the threat of labor on the Sabbath, the poor lived for at least one day a week with the same kind of freedom that the rich enjoyed. The Sabbath, in other words, is God's gift to the dignity of all humankind. It forces us to concentrate on who we are rather than on what we do.

The second reason for the Sabbath, the rabbis say, is to lead us to evaluate our work. As God did on the seventh day, we are also asked to determine whether or not what we are doing in life is really "good." Good for ourselves, good for the people around us, good for the development of the world. But if that is true, then the reason we have nuclear bombs and pornographic movies and underpaid workers may be precisely because we have lost respect for the concept of Sabbath. I mean, how long has it really been since you sat down, thought what your life is about and asked yourself if the work you do is really, really "good" work?

The third reason for the Sabbath, the Hebrew tradition teaches us, is very unlike the American compulsion to turn Sunday into more of the same–only louder, faster and longer. Sabbath is to lead us to reflect on life itself–where we've been, where we're going and why. Sabbath time takes quiet and serious thought and a search for meaning.

Let's see now: If God built rest into the human cycle for one day out of every seven, or 52 days a year, or 3,640 days in the average life-span of 70 years or about ten years out of every lifetime, I'm confused. Tell me again: Why are you tired?

How long has it been since you've taken a day simply to reflect on the way you live–how fast, how balanced, how sensible, how realistic is it? The sad thing is that too often we choose to fret about life rather than reflect on it. We choose to worry about what might happen next instead of deciding what it is that should happen next.

Response: Choose one Soul Point and write three questions it raises in you.

Photo Prayer

Pray the psalm verse to yourself several times.
Now pray with the photo.

Response: What does this photo have to do with the psalm verse,

Be still and know that I am God.
Psalm 46

Looking out the window on a weekday morning, the Hasidic teacher, Nachman of Bratzlav, noticed his disciple, Chaim, rushing along the street.

Reb Nachman opened the window and invited Chaim to come inside. Chaim entered the home and Nachman said to him, "Chaim, have you seen the sky this morning?" "No, Rebbe," answered Chaim. "Have you seen the street this morning?" "Yes, Rebbe." "Tell me, please, Chaim, what did you see in the street?" "I saw people, carts, and merchandise. I saw merchants and peasants all coming and going, selling and buying."

"Chaim," said Nachman, "in 50 years, in 100 years, on that very street there will be a market. Other vehicles will then bring merchants and merchandise to the street. But I won't be here and neither will you. So, I ask you Chaim, what's the good of rushing if you don't even have time to look at the sky?"

Story from *Gates of Shabbat: A Guide for Observing Shabbat*
by Central Conference of American Rabbis

Response: What does this story have to do with the psalm,

Be still
and know that I am God.

Psalm 46

Wisdom Notes

Pray the psalm verse to yourself several times.
Now read the Wisdom Notes and respond.

A society that gives to one class all the opportunities for leisure,
and to another all the burdens of work,
dooms both classes to spiritual sterility.
Lewis Mumford

Sunday clears away the rust of the whole week.
Joseph Addison

Anybody can observe the Sabbath
but making it holy surely takes the rest of the week.
Alice Walker

Leisure consists in all those virtuous activities by which we grow morally,
intellectually and spiritually. It is that which makes a life worth living.
Cicero

A great pianist was once asked by an ardent admirer:
How do you handle the notes as well as you do?
The artist answered: The notes I handled better than many pianists,
but the pauses between the notes–ah! that is where the art resides.
Likrat Shabbat

Response: Copy your favorite Wisdom Note. Why did you choose that one?

Personal Reflection

Write the psalm verse from memory.
Say it aloud.

At this point in my life, this psalm verse

Action

Take at least one "Sabbath moment" each day by stopping and praying, "Be still
and know that I am God."

Window Twenty

Scripture Reading

Day after day takes up the story;
night after night takes up the message.

Psalm 19

Read and memorize the psalm verse.
Pray it over and over again throughout the day
until it comes without effort, until it becomes part of you.

Reflection

Pray the psalm verse to yourself thoughtfully several times.
Now read the Reflection and Response suggestion.

The past is not where we live. Those who cling to it–either its joys or its pains–deny themselves the possibilities of the present.

At the same time, those who are not nourished by the past deny themselves good measure by which to build a new future.

Wherever we are today, the past is some explanation for it. But the past is no reason to continue anything in the present unless there is still enough energy in it to make what we are doing today necessary, worthwhile.

Generation after generation we tell ourselves the stories of the past, the tasks of the present and the promise of the future. Each of them is measured by the eternal truths in the human heart, the call of God that rumbles through the world. This tension between past experiences, the wisdom of the ages and the underlying urgency of now, leaves us with the spiritual balancing act of all time.

Lord Halifax wrote, "Education is what remains after we have forgotten all we have been taught." It is the need for change that challenges tradition and it is tradition that makes change without apocalypse possible.

What is left over after the process concludes itself is called life. Balancing the two is like walking a greased tightrope over Niagara Falls.

Response: Here's an idea. Write down four things that you do every year.
Then, write down why you do them and what you get out of them. That's holy tradition. Yours.

Soul Points

Pray the psalm verse to yourself several times.
Now read the Soul Points by Joan Chittister and respond.

Tradition is the glue of a community. Think about that one for awhile. To give an example: Tradition is what keeps a family coming together on Thanksgiving when, without it, warring brothers and sisters would never want to be in the same room together again for as long as they lived. It keeps us in contact until we're finally ready to discover how much we love one another.

☞

Change tests tradition. Any tradition that can't absorb change could not have been tradition in the first place.

☞

Things like male dominance and white power and female subordination are not "tradition," though many a religious figure argue so. They are simply long-lasting social practices which, based on bad biology, became theology as time went by. These must now give sway to new information and enlightened understanding. Otherwise, bleeding a person would still be basic medical practice, the sun would still revolve around the earth, Indians would still be half-souled and church government would still be the law of the land because once we thought those things were part of the natural law. To blame God for things of human design, to call revelation what are simply long-lived practices derived on the basis of limited data is the worst tradition of them all.

☞

Tradition is meant to be created anew, every single day. Otherwise, tradition becomes a rut instead of the ongoing revelation of God through every time in every people.

☞

"The tragedy of life is that people do not change," Agatha Christie wrote. I'm convinced that's true. I'm also convinced, however, that it is just as much a tragedy when they do change–without being grounded in the past, without a sense of purpose for the future.

Response: Choose one Soul Point and write three questions it raises in you.

Photo Prayer

Pray the psalm verse to yourself several times.
Now pray with the photo.

Response: What does this photo have to do with the psalm verse,

Day after day
takes up the story;
night after night
makes known the message.

Psalm 19

Story

Pray the psalm verse to yourself several times.
Now read the story and respond.

As the roof was leaking, a Zen Master told two monks to bring something to catch the water. One brought a tub, the other a basket. The first was severely reprimanded, the second highly praised.

Response: What does this story have to do with the psalm,

Day after day takes up the story;
night after night makes known the message.

Psalm 19

Wisdom Notes

Pray the psalm verse to yourself several times.
Now read the Wisdom Notes and respond.

It is not that I belong to the past, but that the past belongs to me.
Mary Antin

To know the road ahead, ask those coming back.
Chinese proverb

The first act of creation is destruction.
e.e. cummings

A society that domesticates its rebels has gained its peace.
But it has lost its future.
Anthony de Mello

Tradition means giving votes to the most obscure of all classes–
our ancestors. It is the democracy of the dead.
Tradition refuses to submit to the small and arrogant oligarchy
of those who merely happen to be walking around.
G.K. Chesterton

Response: Copy your favorite Wisdom Note. Why did you choose that one?

Personal Reflection

Write the psalm verse from memory.
Say it aloud.

At this point in my life, this psalm verse

_____

Action

Start a scrapbook or Tradition Memoir that explains the traditions you grew up with in your family. Then give the book to your grandchildren, nieces, nephews, great-grandchildren, your own children, etc. as a gift for a birthday or Christmas.

Window Twenty-one

Scripture Reading

*It is good to proclaim your love
in the morning
And your truth in the watches of the night.*

Psalm 92

**Read and memorize the psalm verse.
Pray it over and over again throughout the day
until it comes without effort, until it becomes part of you.**

Reflection

**Pray the psalm verse to yourself thoughtfully several times.
Now read the Reflection and Response suggestion.**

Some people ask, "How are we supposed to pray?" Other people ask—more correctly, I think—"How do *you* pray?" Prayer, you see, is a very personal part of spiritual development. It changes as we change. It deepens as we grow, simplifies as we do, as the years go by.

Prayer centers us and stretches us and lays us bare, as the prayer says, "of all self-conceits." Inside ourselves, we know who we are and what we need and what we lack and what we don't understand and what we long for as we go. It is this awareness and the dependence on God it brings with it that are the wellspring of prayer.

Those thoughts, if we honor them and face them, become the function of a prayer life that will eventually strip us of everything but our desire for God. Prayer is the awareness that it is not a question of whether or not God is present to us—that we can take for granted; instead, prayer is the process of *our* becoming present to God.

So, real prayer can be fed by any one of a number of things—Scripture, nature, personal experience, emotional pressures, intellectual commitment to the God who is greater than any idea of God we can possibly have. But whatever the life-link that brings us into consciousness of God, in the end the way we pray has something to do with who we are.

The whole notion, then, that there is some prayer formula or ritual or schedule or style that is right for everyone is, at best, naïve. Even *The Rule of Benedict*, that sixth-century document on the spiritual life that devotes more chapters to prayer than to any other topic in *The Rule*, ends the long outline of psalms and readings by saying, "But if any of the monastics know a better way, let them arrange them differently." No single form, we find, is the ultimate valuation of a life of prayer.

Prayer is real if it changes us, if it enables the inbreaking of God in our lives. And to do that we must "proclaim your love in the morning…your truth in the watches of the night."

Excerpt taken from the Foreword by Joan Chittister in PRAYING WITH THE BENEDICTINES by Guerric DeBona, OSB. Copyright ©2006. Reprinted with permission of Paulist Press, Inc., New York/Mahwah, NJ www.paulistpress.com.

Response: For 15 minutes sit someplace without work, without television, without music. Just sit.

Soul Points

Pray the psalm verse to yourself several times.
Now read the Soul Points by Joan Chittister and respond.

Prayer erupts in the heart at the sight of either the impossibly beautiful or the unbearably difficult. It is, in both cases, a signal of the breakthrough of the divine into the mundane.

When we have prayed prayers long enough, all the words drop away and we begin to live in the presence of God. Then prayer is finally real.

Every time we pray we come one step closer, not to changing God, but to converting ourselves.

Prayer is not a magic act; it is a relationship that calls the spiritual dimension in us to life, that attunes us to the universe, that hears the sound of the great I Am everywhere.

Reminder in a church bulletin: "Let us remember in prayer the many who are sick of our church and community." It's hard to know who to pray for in a situation like that. It must be tough for God, too.

Response: Choose one Soul Point and write three questions it raises in you.

Photo Prayer

Pray the psalm verse to yourself several times.
Now pray with the photo.

Response: What does this photo have to do with the psalm verse,

It is good to proclaim your love
in the morning
And your truth
in the watches of the night.

Psalm 92

Pray the psalm verse to yourself several times.
Now read the story and respond.

A cobbler came to Rabbi Isaac of Ger and said, "Tell me what to do about my morning prayer. My customers are poor men who have only one pair of shoes. I pick up their shoes late in the evening and work on them most of the night; at dawn there is still work to be done if the men are to have their shoes ready before they go to work. Now my question is, What should I do about my morning prayer?"

"What have you been doing till now?" the Rabbi asked.

"Sometimes I rush through the prayer quickly and get back to my work–but then I feel bad about it. At other times I let the hour of prayer go by. Then too I feel a sense of loss and every now and then, as I raise my hammer from the shoes, I can almost hear my heart sigh, 'What an unlucky man I am, that I am not able to make my morning prayer.'"

Said the Rabbi, "If I were God I would value that sigh more than the prayer."

from *Taking Flight* by Anthony de Mello, SJ

Response: What does this story have to do with the psalm,

It is good to proclaim your love
in the morning
And your truth
in the watches of the night.

Psalm 92

Wisdom Notes

Pray the psalm verse to yourself several times.
Now read the Wisdom Notes and respond.

Pray to God but continue to row to shore.
Russian proverb

I have lived to thank God that all my prayers have not been answered.
Jean Ingelow

Never pray in a room without windows.
The Talmud

The higher goal of spiritual living is not to amass a wealth of information,
but to face sacred moments.
Rabbi Abraham Heshel

Jesus went out to a lonely place where he prayed.
Mark 1:35

Response: Copy your favorite Wisdom Note. Why did you choose that one?

Personal Reflection

Write the psalm verse from memory.
Say it aloud.

At this point in my life, this psalm verse

_____

Action

Try a different form of prayer for one week: chant with a CD; sit in silence for
20 minutes and repeat a prayer silently or repeat a holy word; say the rosary;
recite a psalm aloud; read a section of Scripture slowly and then reflect on it;
listen to your favorite hymns, etc. There are many prayer aids on the web.

Window Twenty-two

Scripture Reading

Give thanks to God.
Tell God's name.

Psalm 105

Read and memorize the psalm verse.
Pray it over and over again throughout the day
until it comes without effort, until it becomes part of you.

Reflection

Pray the psalm verse to yourself thoughtfully several times.
Now read the Reflection and Response suggestion.

This psalm is a history psalm. It tells a story of life's pain and mystery and God's salvation. It reminds us of the trials of Abraham, Isaac, Jacob, Joseph, Moses, Aaron. Finally we realize what's being said: In the long run, whatever things God allows to happen to us are right.

Every difficulty is an opportunity, a call, not for rescue but for personal growth. We have to learn to accept the will of God in our own lives and be faithful under all circumstances, good and bad. God works through both for our good and growth. We like the good but cannot tolerate the bad.

Consequently, we often fail to look at trouble with the perspective that faith brings. We fail to look under what troubles us to discover its meaning and its challenge. We fail to ask ourselves, how can I grow from this?

All things come from God's hand. God is working in our lives even when we can't see that. Those are situations we all have and all understand. They are not easy but those are the things that call us to sanctity, too.

That's a good lesson. We get so bogged down in the immediate, the daily, that we forget the full shape of our lives. Everyone has a history and story of pain, yet in all of it we have been saved. Out of every bad thing comes good, comes growth, if we allow it. That's important to remember every new time that our worlds seem to end.

So our history, too, tells us to "give thanks to God; tell God's name;" spread hope and faith, not despair and discontent.

Response: Name one thing that happened to you recently which you thought at first was bad but which turned out to be for your good.

Soul Points

Pray the psalm verse to yourself several times.
Now read the Soul Points by Joan Chittister and respond.

Life is a relentless teacher. And life teaches relentlessly.

The myth of life lived on an even keel persists in the minds of many, but seduces only the weak of heart.

The wounds of life are what make for the scar tissue of the soul. And scar tissue is always stronger than normal tissue.

We don't create our destinies; we only shape them.

Life lies in taking all the pieces of our lives, considering what has been the function of each and growing beyond them to the person we want to be now.

Response: Choose one Soul Point and write three questions it raises in you.

Photo Prayer

Pray the psalm verse to yourself several times.
Now pray with the photo.

Give thanks to God.
Tell God's name.

Psalm 105

Response: What does this photo have to do with the psalm verse?

Pray the psalm verse to yourself several times.
Now read the story and respond.

Once there was a farmer whose only horse escaped the corral. When his neighbors lamented his loss, the farmer said, "Good event, bad event, who knows?"

But when the horse returned to the farm leading a whole herd of wild horses with him the neighbors congratulated the old man on his luck. Then, the farmer said, "Good event, bad event, who knows?"

Later, when the farmer's only son was thrown from the back of the horse and broke his leg at harvest time, the neighbors bewailed his troubles. But the farmer said, "Good event, bad event, who knows?"

And when the warlord conscripted every young man in the valley for his army except the boy with the broken leg, the other farmers whose sons had been taken, cursed their bad luck and celebrated his fortune. But the farmer said, "Good event, bad event, who knows?"

A Chinese Tale

Response: What does this story have to do with the psalm,

Give thanks to God.
Tell God's name.

Psalm 105

Wisdom Notes

Pray the psalm verse to yourself several times.
Now read the Wisdom Notes and respond.

No one is more unhappy than the one who is never in adversity;
the greatest affliction of life is never to be afflicted at all.
Book of Proverbs

There are joys which long to be ours. God sends ten thousand truths,
which come about us like birds seeking inlet; but we are shut up to them,
and so they bring us nothing, but sit and sing awhile upon the roof,
and then fly away.
Henry Ward Beecher

A wounded deer leaps highest.
Emily Dickinson

Lives that flash in sunshine, and lives that are born in tears,
receive their hue from circumstances.
Harriet Jacobs

(Be) resolved to take Fate by the throat and shake a living out of her.
Louisa Mae Alcott

Response: Copy your favorite Wisdom Note. Why did you choose that one?

Personal Reflection

Write the psalm verse from memory.
Say it aloud.

At this point in my life, this psalm verse

Action

On a sheet of paper write "I give thanks to you, my God" on ten lines. Now
finish the prayer by thanking God for five "good" events and five "bad" events
in your life. Share your prayer of gratitude with a close friend.

Window
Twenty-three

Scripture Reading

*God saves
a humble people.*

Psalm 18

Read and memorize the psalm verse.
Pray it over and over again throughout the day
until it comes without effort, until it becomes part of you.

Reflection

Pray the psalm verse to yourself thoughtfully several times.
Now read the Reflection and Response suggestion.

This is a good psalm for beginning any difficult thing. It brings an important insight to any moment of risk or uncertainty or pressure. The message is stark and clear: God saves a humble people, those for whom God is God.

Humility, after all, is simply the truth of our own existence. Humility is the ability to know at all times who we are in the universe. Humility lets God be God.

The humble are those who don't have to control everything. The humble are those who don't have to have reasons for everything. The humble are those who don't have to be sure of everything. The humble are those who simply do their best and then let life take its course. They let things happen. They let schedules and work and plans and people go their own way because they trust others and they trust God.

Then God can work in their lives. Then they can allow change knowing, "God saves a humble people."

Response: Today—just for one day—let everything happen the way other people suggest. Evaluate the day. What happened to it? What happened to you?

Soul Points

People who are really humble, who know themselves to be earth or *humus*–the root from which our word humble comes–have about themselves an air of self-containment and self-control.

Humility is the total continuing surrender to God's power in my life and in the lives of those around me.

The humble person gives all their special gifts away–their ideas, their time, their talents, their presence–and is genuinely surprised to discover that other people really want them.

Humility is the ability to recognize the glory in the clay of me.

Humility saves us from the terminal disease of self-centeredness. It enables us to be comfortable with who we are so that we can be comfortable with who everyone else is, too.

Response: Choose one Soul Point and write three questions it raises in you.

Photo Prayer

Pray the psalm verse to yourself several times.
Now pray with the photo.

Response: What does this photo have to do with the psalm,

God saves a humble people.

Psalm 18

Story

**Pray the psalm verse to yourself several times.
Now read the story and respond.**

I walked up to an old, old monk and asked him, "What
is the audacity of humility?" This man had never met me before,
but do you know what his answer was? "To be the first to say,
'I love you.'"

from *The Tales of the Magic Monastery*
by Theophane the Monk

Response: What does this story have to do with the psalm,

*God saves
a humble people.*

Psalm 18

Wisdom Notes

Pray the psalm verse to yourself several times.
Now read the Wisdom Notes and respond.

Without humility there can be no humanity.
John Buchan

If you bow at all, bow low.
Chinese proverb

Remember that you are dust and unto dust you shall return.
Ash Wednesday prayer

I believe that the first test of a truly great person is humility.
John Ruskin

Anybody can be Pope; the proof of this is that I have become one.
Pope John XXIII

Response: Copy your favorite Wisdom Note. Why did you choose that one?

Personal Reflection

Write the psalm verse from memory.
Say it aloud.

At this point in my life, this psalm verse

_____

Action

Say "I love you" to someone today, a person who least expects it. Tell them why you love them.

Window
Twenty-four

Scripture Reading

The heavens are yours,
the earth is yours;
The world and its fullness,
you have made.

Psalm 89

Read and memorize the psalm verse.
Pray it over and over again throughout the day
until it comes without effort, until it becomes part of you.

Reflection

Pray the psalm verse to yourself thoughtfully several times.
Now read the Reflection and Response suggestion.

This is a psalm about relationships. It is rich with the promise and the responsibilities that go with a covenant with God. It reminds us that we are the stewards, not the owners of this creation.

The trouble comes when we forget that, when we begin to think that all the things in life belong to us. We talk about "our staff" and "our projects" and "our money" and "our car" and "our land" and "our success" and "our achievements." We begin to own God's works and ownership of God's works leads inevitably to downfall and disappointment because the center shifts. We begin to think about control instead of human community and the purpose of life and the real meaning of things. The psalm asks for a spirit of co-creation. It asks us to let go.

Response: Try to get through today without saying my or mine.

Soul Points

We must begin to see the planet as something with a life of its own, holy and filled with the glory of God.

We have made war on nature and wonder why there is so little peace in ourselves when, what we destroy, is exactly what we need most.

To be immersed in nature is to be immersed in the imagination of God.

We do not exist outside of nature or above nature or independent of nature; we are simply its most vulnerable part.

Responsibility for life is what the modern world has most lost. In a throwaway society, nothing is seen as having life. Things have simply a temporary usefulness.

Response: Choose one Soul Point and write three questions it raises in you.

Photo Prayer

Pray the psalm verse to yourself several times.
Now pray with the photo.

Response: What does this photo have to do with the psalm verse,

The heavens are yours,
the earth is yours;
the world and its fullness you have made.

Psalm 89

Story
**Pray the psalm verse to yourself several times.
Now read the story and respond.**

"There are three stages in one's spiritual development,"
said the Master: "the carnal, the spiritual and the divine."

"Well, Master," the eager disciples asked, "what is the
carnal stage?"

"That's the stage when trees are seen as trees and mountains
as mountains," the Master answered.

"And the spiritual?" the disciples continued.

"The spiritual is when one looks more deeply into things.
Then trees are no longer trees and mountains no longer mountains."

"And the divine?" the disciples asked in awe.

"Ah, yes, the divine," the Master said and chuckled, "is when
the trees become trees again and mountains, mountains."

Response: What does this story have to do with the psalm,

*The heavens are yours,
the earth is yours;
the world and its fullness
you have made.*

Psalm 89

Wisdom Notes

Pray the psalm verse to yourself several times.
Now read the Wisdom Notes and respond.

You have to see God and creation all together
and see God in creation and creation in God and don't ever separate them.
Then everything manifests God instead of hiding God
or being in the way of God as an obstacle.
Thomas Merton

Arranging a bowl of flowers in the morning can give a sense of quiet
in a crowded day—like writing a poem or saying a prayer.
Anne Morrow Lindbergh

Those who contemplate the beauty of the earth
find reserves of strength
that will endure as long as life lasts.
Rachel Carson

We are earth of this earth, and we are bone of its bone, /
This is a prayer I sing, for we have forgotten this and so /
The earth is perishing.
Barbara Deming

I am two with nature.
Woody Allen

Response: Copy your favorite Wisdom Note. Why did you choose that one?

Personal Reflection

Write the psalm verse from memory.
Say it aloud.

At this point in my life, this psalm verse

Action

Make a nature date with yourself. Once a week go and enjoy some natural scene—a lake, forest, garden, sunset.

Window
Twenty-five

Scripture Reading

Your love is better than life.
My soul is filled as with a banquet;
My soul is full of joy.

Psalm 63

Read and memorize the psalm verse.
Pray it over and over again throughout the day
until it comes without effort, until it becomes part of you.

Reflection

Pray the psalm verse to yourself thoughtfully several times.
Now read the Reflection and Response suggestion.

"I learn by going where I have to go," Theodore Roetke wrote. And that's an important concept. All of life cannot be planned. Our life is God's and gratitude is its key.

Giving thanks to God is good psychologically to keep our thoughts light and full of energy. It is not true, psychologists tell us, that we think the way we feel. On the contrary, we feel the way we think and thoughts can be changed.

Giving thanks to God is good spiritually. That is the beginning of contemplation.

Giving thanks to God is good socially. It makes us a positive presence in a group. (Only negative people want to be around negative people.)

We need to stop and thank God—consciously—for the good things of the day. We spend so much time wanting things to be better that we fail to see our real gifts. There are banquets in our life and we don't enjoy them because we are always grasping for something more: the perfect schedule, the perfect work, the perfect friend, the perfect community. We have to realize that God's gifts are all around us, that joy is an attitude of mind, an awareness that my life is basically good. Dissatisfaction is too often a sign of something wrong in me.

As the Eastern mystic says: "O wonder of wonders: I chop wood; I draw water from the well."

Response: Whatever the weather is—hot, rainy, cold, windy—go out and stand in it for 10 minutes. Let it affect you. What good came from the experience?

Soul Points

Only the ordinary makes the special, special. To be glutted with specialness is to lose all sense of the exceptional in life.

⟨

The ordinary is what reveals to us, little by little, inch by inch, "the holiness of life, before which," Dag Hammerskjöld wrote, "we bow down in worship."

⟨

To the real mystic, the passing of the seasons is never commonplace. It is the repetition that finally, finally opens our eyes to God where God has always been: right under the feet of us.

⟨

If I cook dinner, that's ordinary. If I put a flower on the table when I serve it, that's divine.

⟨

Coming to be fully alive is the task of a lifetime. There's so much in each of us that we have never touched, so much beauty we're steeped in that we've overlooked. Consciousness is what lifts the ordinary to the level of the sublime.

Response: Choose one Soul Point and write three questions it raises in you.

Photo Prayer

Pray the psalm verse to yourself several times.
Now pray with the photo

Response: What does this photo have to do with the psalm verse,

Your love is better than life.
My soul is filled as with a banquet;
My life is full of joy.

Psalm 63

**Pray the psalm verse to yourself several times.
Now read the story and respond.**

A rabbi in a dream found himself in Heaven.

"Where is Paradise?" he asked. So they showed him a room where many spiritual leaders were sitting around a table absorbed in the Scriptures.

"Is this, then, all there is to Paradise?" he queried in disappointment.

"You do not understand," they said to him. "The sages are not in Paradise. Paradise is in the sages."

Tales of the Hasidim

Response: What does this story have to do with the psalm,

Your love is better than life.
My soul is filled as with a banquet;
My life is full of joy.

Psalm 63

Wisdom Notes

Pray the psalm verse to yourself several times.
Now read the Wisdom Notes and respond.

How we spend our days is, of course,
how we spend our lives.
Annie Dillard

To live is to be slowly born.
Antoine de Saint-Exupéry

There are more truths in twenty-four hours
than in all the philosophies.
Raoul Vaneigem

A cow must graze where it is tied.
African proverb

O wonder of wonders:
I chop wood; I draw water from the well.
Zen saying

Response: Copy your favorite Wisdom Note. Why did you choose that one?

Personal Reflection

Write the psalm verse from memory.
Say it aloud.

At this point in my life, this psalm verse

Action

Make it a practice to say "thank you" at least once a day to God and to another person. Be specific when you say "thank you." Do this for a month and then evaluate the impact, if any, of this spiritual practice on your life.

Photo Credits

Art Becker—Cover, 7, 47, 62, 72, 112, 117, 122

Ed Bernick—Back Cover

Carolyn Gorny-Kopkowski, OSB—12, 37

Claire Hudert, OSB—42, 67

Mary Miller, OSB—82, 87,127

Ann Muczynski, OSB—27

Margaret Ann Pilewski, OSB—17, 77

Stephanie Schmidt, OSB—22, 52, 92, 97, 102

Bernadette Sullivan, OSB—107

Lucia Marie Surmik, OSB—57

Marian Wehler, OSB—32